THE LIFE OF SIR ENOCH HILL

SIR ENOCH HILL

THE LIFE OF
SIR ENOCH HILL

*The Romance of the Modern
Building Society*

by

R. K. BACON

General Editor of this Series
COLLIN BROOKS

LONDON
IVOR NICHOLSON & WATSON, LTD.
44 ESSEX STREET, STRAND, W.C.2
1934

FIRST EDITION . MAY 1934

PRINTED IN GREAT BRITAIN BY
JARROLD AND SONS LIMITED,
THE EMPIRE PRESS, NORWICH

GENERAL EDITOR'S INTRODUCTION

THE purpose of this series of biographies is three-fold. It is the intention, first, to tell the stories of men who, by the exercise of strong personal initiative and marked qualities, have risen in the community to positions that are not only commanding but directional. The romances of their careers, it is hoped, may stimulate the initiative and industry of a younger generation. Were this the sole intention, however, the series would be little better than a modern parody of the famous "Self-help" lives of Samuel Smiles. The second intention is to reveal the power which a forceful character has to shape the lives of the community outside the political field. The third intention is to display some of the incentives and rewards which modern capitalism offers to those who find in private enterprise a medium for the exercise of their powers.

The selection of Sir Enoch Hill as the first subject of the series is not accidental. His life story is as romantic as any of our generation, and the work which has absorbed him—that of increasing the number of property owners by providing a channel for thrift—stands in a special relation to the economic flux of his time.

Mr. R. K. Bacon has brought to the writing of Sir Enoch Hill's story a fitting objectivity. The society which bred the man, the man himself, and the organisation which he has created are all given a fitting perspective. The gravest danger in the writing of such a biography is that both subject and biographer may appear unpleasantly "smug". This danger Mr. Bacon has avoided.

The life of Sir Enoch begins with a hard-working family in a textile industry, a harassed mother, and a child condemned to early labour: it ends with a generous host entertaining his guest in a comfortable and dignified home over three centuries old. But if any imagine that this sweep from material hardship to material affluence contains the whole significance of Sir Enoch Hill's career, Mr. Bacon's book will correct the error. If any imagine that private enterprise and individualism mean only such satisfactions as may come from "gathering gear"—again, Mr. Bacon's book, and those to follow it, will correct the error.

If any potential reader fears that such a biography can be only a dull chronicle, let him be assured that here, in essence, is such a story as Arnold Bennett might have written—as some future Bennett may, indeed, on the foundation here laid for him, come to write.

C. B.

ACKNOWLEDGMENTS

THE author's thanks are due to the Editors of the *Yorkshire Evening Post* and the *Halifax Courier* for permission to quote from articles which they have published; and to Mr. F. Emmett (Halifax Building Society), Mr. W. A. Smith (Kettering), Mr. Jabez Crabtree (Keighley), Dr. J. M. Johnston (Medical Officer of Health for Leek), Mr. A. H. Moore, J.P. (Leek), and Mrs. A. C. Mee (Leek) for information and assistance generously given.

CONTENTS

AUTHOR'S PREFACE

BIOGRAPHY is a vast presumption. That is why the Anglo-Saxon race, which is modest by nature, has made but few outstanding contributions to the art. Fortunately for the biographer, it is only of famous or infamous people he is called upon to write. And he tells us not what they are or were—for that is quite beyond his power—but what they did or said or, when he is very bold, what he thinks they thought. It is not his fault. Human personality is a subjective affair, and it is only with its reflections and not the thing itself that he can deal. So the biography of the ordinary man—the Mr. Pooters who make up the run of mankind—will never be written. The exposure would be too great. As in any case most of us are Pooters, we know enough about him without wanting to read more. So, tacitly acknowledging the wisdom of the dispensation that limits the biographer's art, we let him escape to his harvest among the great and the illustrious.

If the biography of Sir Enoch Hill should fail in aught, the fault must be with the biographer, for Hill himself is one who has the biographical qualifications *in excelsis*. He has done things which no man has done before—things which have contributed not merely to the success of his own life but to the well-being and contentment of his countrymen. It is a tenet of capitalist philosophy that no one can prosper without helping others, though some have striven diligently to shake this faith. The example of Enoch Hill is a powerful restorative. Surmounting almost incredible obstacles, he has become the protagonist of the movement that has spread the gospel of home-ownership throughout the land—his success the success of an organisation that bestrides the Building Society world like a colossus. To him more than to any other man belongs the credit for having broken down the distinction between the few who owned houses and the many who merely lived in them.

Considered as a redistribution of wealth, the change is significant enough, but not more so than the general growth of the small capitalist class ; it is in the quality rather than the extent of the new ownership that the social momentousness of Sir Enoch's life must be observed. It is not *a* house which the Building Society enables a man to buy but, for the most part, *the* house which is his home. An immense contribution has thus been made to the creation throughout the land of a better home environment, the supreme importance of which to the life of the rising generation has been made manifest by analytical psychology.

In one sense the Building Society movement is the result of thrift, co-operation and compound interest, a thing of loans and mortgage deeds. These, it is true, are its constituent parts, but from their combination a new entity has emerged, purposive, creative, and conscious of its significance. We may call this emergent quality an awareness of immense capacity to serve the social organism. And Sir Enoch Hill worked his miracle because, above all else, he personified this quality. An ambitious man, this—but it is ambition with a noble strain. Poverty and suffering left him unafraid, wealth and success unspoilt. Of him it may be said, as it was of Marcus Aurelius, that he knew how to lack and how to enjoy those things in the lack whereof most men show themselves weak and in the fruition intemperate.

R. K. B.

LEEDS
January 1934

THE LIFE OF SIR ENOCH HILL

CHAPTER I

THE ROUGH ROAD

A CAPACITY for sustained work, cheerful courage and a contemplative faculty rare in men of action are undoubtedly the attributes to which, in the life of Enoch Hill, personal success and a fine record of national service owe their origin and completion. The mill-hand's child working in a mill at eight years old, who now at sixty-eight is President of the greatest Building Society in the world, ex-Chairman of the National Association of Building Societies, a newspaper owner, a power in the worlds of finance and social service, did not rise from so lowly to so exalted a place on any foundation less sound than remarkable native worth and ability. At work at eight years of age, and to-day at sixty-eight still working, affords, perhaps, the clue to the rest. Without continuous and hard work certainly no success so worthy could have been achieved; but to energy were added vision, courage to take any corner, and an imaginative and kindly realisation of the needs of others. This last may explain why the spirit of the youth facing an uncompromising necessity to earn a living found its true orientation, when the youth had grown to manhood, in helping forward one of the greatest social movements of the age.

The parents of Enoch Hill, Henry and Elizabeth

2   17

Hill, began their married life in Ball Haye Green, Leek, Staffordshire, on the strategic assumption that two together can live as cheaply as one. Both were employed in the indigenous trade of silk spinning, and wife as well as husband continued to work after marriage, until the time came when Elizabeth had to exchange for a while her toil at the mill for the labour of childbirth. Enoch, the first of a family of seven, was born on September 10, 1865. During the next ten years, while the family was growing, Elizabeth, with the inexplicable strength and tenacity which mothers of poor families seem infinitely to possess, conjoined the duties of housewifery and motherhood with nine hours of work daily at the silk-spinning frames. This mother had few material gifts to disperse to her family, but her resolute character, endurance and capacity for arduous toil compounded for her children a richer inheritance than gold.

It was a household in which stern necessity was chief guide, and Enoch, as the eldest of a growing family whose income was stationary as well as meagre, was called upon to help in the wage-earning while still a child. On his eighth birthday Enoch sought and found a job, and it was an adventurous and independent young man who, at that tender age, set out to join the ranks of the millworkers. He was proud to begin making an active contribution to the family exchequer —although as a half-timer his wage was no more than a shilling for a week's work—and possibly, also, the pride was sweetened for the lawgiver to younger brothers and sisters (for he had been his mother's nursemaid and housemaid from earliest recollection) by thought of the still greater prestige he was now able to assume.

But, according to the standard of that time, beginning work meant practically the end of school education for Enoch. The progress of industrial legislation in the nineteenth century had been painfully slow. Although the first Factory Act was passed in 1802 and the first legislative restrictions imposed on the employment of children in 1819, juvenile labour in textile factories was still widespread half a century later. The lowness of wages placed parents in urgent need of the pittances their children could earn, and they resisted efforts to restrict the scope of such employment. In 1873, when Enoch Hill set out to his first job, children under twelve years of age were still permitted to work half time, though the other half was in theory devoted to education. Child workers had become known as "half-timers". The fiction that an improperly fed child was fit, after more than four hours of manual work, to proceed to acquire knowledge—except perhaps of that kind which "by suffering entereth"—was, it is true, never regarded very seriously. By putting in an appearance at school once a week it was possible for a child to obtain a certificate of regular attendance, and of this convenience Enoch and his parents, in common with thousands more, were glad to avail themselves.

So, no longer troubled by school attendance, Enoch

directed undivided attention to his first job, which was in a garret workshop run by a woman named Mears. His task was to turn the wheel of a manual engine which provided power for the silk-winding frames in the workshop. It was not so long before that Mrs. Elizabeth Barrett Browning, in " The Cry of the Children", had written:

> All day the iron wheels go onward
>   Grinding life down from its mark;
> And the children's souls, which God is calling sunward,
>   Shine on blindly in the dark.

That a child should escape with his spirit unimpaired from the monotony of turning a wheel for four and a half hours daily on six days a week is not a little surprising when we consider the efforts now made by industrial psychologists to palliate the consequences of such labour on workers of a much more mature age. But the risks, if recognised at all by Enoch's parents, failed to weigh in the balance against the shilling a week which he earned. It is probable that young Hill was just about as impervious to hardship as any human being can be; it was hardship nevertheless from the consequences of which only a rare spirit could have escaped.

Enoch next found a job at two shillings a week. He had still to turn a wheel, but this time a much bigger one. Then in a larger mill he became a bobbin carrier—a definite move up in the scale of juvenile employment—and was paid half a crown a week.

The need to make a bigger contribution to the family income was at this time always in the forefront of his mind, and he was therefore ever on the look-out for means of adding to his meagre wages. He sold newspapers in the streets, ran casual errands for shop-keepers, and earned occasional extras by soliciting orders for Christmas gifts and hot-cross buns, and subsequently delivering the goods around the district. He was watchful also for loads of coal dumped, as was the practice, in the channel near the causeway in front of houses. For shovelling a ton into the coal-house he charged the competitive price of sixpence. And so he found it possible, by dint of careful manage-ment, to save a few shillings for the Leek May Fair and provide a treat for his brothers and sisters—with whom his prestige was thus further enhanced. An old resident of Leek is fond of telling how Enoch used to take his brothers and sisters on the roundabouts and swings and to all the shows as long as his money lasted, never failing to save fourpence to take a pie back for his father and mother's fairing.

Many years later, Sir Enoch saw some hungry-looking children gazing into a cookshop window with longing eyes. He remembered the joy of his brothers and sisters when treated to cookshop hospitality, and he had the idea of giving each of the children a shilling and telling them to buy something to eat. He did so. The children looked at their shillings and at each other, and finally at the giver. The first to find his tongue turned to his companions and enquired in awestruck tones, "Is he soft?" But the generosity of the older Enoch Hill was rooted in the necessity of the youngsters.

On reaching the age of thirteen, Enoch qualified for full-time employment without even the formality of attending an elementary school for one half day per week. He was strong and active by this time, with a capacity for endurance which many a man would have envied. He therefore did not hesitate to seek the hardest—and so the best paid—job available to a lad working whole-time in the silk trade, that of a twister's helper. For this plum of employment the wage was no less than nine shillings per week—for those who survived.

Enoch's own father was a silk twister. The work consisted of twisting silk yarns by hand power, the helper being a boy who unreeled the sections of yarn for twisting in extended lengths. Under the piecework scale which usually operated, it was possible for a skilled man to earn about thirty shillings a week. But to reach this figure meant persistent work for nine and a half hours a day, and the poor helper, who was personally employed by the twister, had to keep up to the pace the twister set. For the helper it meant interminable journeys backwards and forwards in bare feet over a wet clay floor, carrying the half-twisted yarn to be doubled and trebled and re-twisted by the man. It was probably the hardest work that ever fell to the lot of Enoch Hill; but even then his chief grudge against it was that it gave him an appetite which the economic exigencies of his home made difficult to satisfy! But, appetite satisfied or not, he remained a twister's helper for three years, and in that time observed an increasing responsibility for the welfare of the younger members of his family.

But the severities of employment had at times to be exchanged for the even greater severities of unemployment and part-time working. The depression which descended upon the country at the close of the Franco-Prussian War caught the silk industry firmly in its grasp. Prices were tumbling, and inevitably the rapid mechanical improvements of the age were blamed for a situation primarily the result of a world movement, led by Germany, towards the Gold Standard, and the consequent growing demand for the metal.

These periods of unemployment, during which the income of the Hill family was reduced almost to vanishing point, left a deep impression on Enoch's mind. But neither in his outlook nor in the atmosphere of his home was there anything of rebellion, or anything of resignation. The Hills had faith that there was always something which could be done to ease the situation, and with an energy that must have been native, as it certainly could not have been derived from the domestic dietary, they set about doing it.

A huge box mangle which occupied the "sitting-room" of their cottage did particularly useful service. This was the kind of mangle that had at its top a chamber filled with stones, the weight of which pressed down the rollers, with good effect upon the clothes if not upon those who turned the handle. Enoch and his father were, in fact, the only members of the family strong enough to turn these rollers. As Mrs. Hill had a reputation for being a thorough worker, she could usually secure a fairly plentiful supply of washing commissions, but the discomfort which this sadly necessary enterprise caused in the sitting-room must have been acute.

For the father to find means to earn some money during slackness at the mills was more difficult, as so many men simultaneously found themselves affected by the same need. But he turned to good account a skill he had acquired in the manufacture of the wire hooks used by silk twisters. These were fashioned from wire $\frac{3}{8}$ in. thick, cut into pieces 7 in. long. Each length was sharpened and tapered by hand and the fine point bent over to form a hook, behind which a shoulder was made by the skilful tap of a hammer. When the hooks had been sand-papered, they were made up into parcels and the father departed to sell them to the factories at a shilling a parcel.

The proceeds were not too great, however, to diminish the eager patronage which the family bestowed upon the soup-kitchens established in the town at such times. One resort beloved of Enoch was a dyeworks where the proprietor converted his vats—normally used for dyeing silk yarns—into receptacles for boiling soup. The children were allowed to take a canful home.

It is perhaps not insignificant that at an early age Enoch ceased to compete for the favours of his parents and himself assumed something of the parental role towards the younger members of the family. The man who has pioneered home-ownership in this country may fittingly have acquired the qualities of heart and mind to inspire a great social movement in himself, having to consider from childhood days the needs of a humble home.

CHAPTER II

WORK AND ROMANCE

ATTRACTIVE as the wage of a twister's helper undoubtedly was, young Hill had ambitions which he could not hope to satisfy in the silk industry of the town. By remaining where he was he could at most emerge eventually as a fully fledged silk twister. He therefore resolved to seek his livelihood in some other way, and his decision was heartily supported by his parents, who by their own experience in the silk mills were well qualified to know what little promise this occupation held for their eldest son. They were by now quite definitely impressed by the boy's restless energy and resourcefulness, and, like many other parents, were anxious that the qualities they discerned should have scope for development. But for people with no money and no influence to seek work "with prospects" for a boy with no education was to undertake a difficult task; and so the Hills found.

Enoch, however, looked around for himself, and at length decided to take a job as a farm labourer. He consequently, at the age of sixteen, said farewell for ever to the silk industry of his native town.

But for the sharp-witted factory lad rusticity proved to have little charm, and he very shortly renewed his search for a congenial occupation.

It was in a printing office at Leek that Enoch eventually found himself as an unindentured apprentice, for the first time in a job which, although humble, gave rein to an alertness of mind and a native curiosity which monotonous labour and lack of education had held severely in check. An arrangement was made for his apprenticeship to spread over a number of years, his wages to begin at five shillings a week, with one shilling per week advance each year.

His first work was that of the ubiquitous printer's devil, and afterwards he became a newsboy, delivering newspapers and periodicals ordered from his employer. Enoch thus renewed acquaintance with walking exercise of a fairly arduous nature, for his work led him first to a railway station a mile away early in the morning, and then, after he had sorted the papers, to all parts of the town for their delivery. Having our papers delivered to our doors free of charge, ready for consumption with the toast and marmalade, was a convenience we owed to the plentiful supply of half-starved and ill-clothed lads ready to go their rounds through every sort of weather for the most miserable of rewards. Hill had the comfort not usually attached to this occupation, that he was working his way towards something better; but even this reflection scarcely kept him warm. He went through the worst of weather coatless until the compassionate wife of a Wesleyan Methodist minister, at whose house he called one wild snowy day to deliver the *Methodist Recorder*, gave him the first overcoat he ever wore. But it was not until he was enveloped in its comfortable folds that he realised how cold he had been without it.

Presently he entered the printing department as apprentice compositor and letterpress printer, and from the primitive equipment in use in the office made his first acquaintance with typography. The few machines were operated by manual labour and all type-setting was done by hand. His employer was a Wesleyan Methodist local preacher, and for this reason as well, no doubt, as for the quality of his work, got a good deal of patronage from the Wesleyan body. The work included the printing of hymn sheets for use at the anniversary services for the various chapels in the circuit. The orders came in late in the week and very often were not completed until Saturday afternoon or evening, involving overtime, which Hill greatly appreciated, not only because of the extra twopence an hour but also because of the bread and butter tea which was provided on Saturday afternoons if work was being carried on into the evening.

Recognising the marked discrepancy in the rates at which his typographical skill and his wages were progressing, Hill terminated his unindentured apprenticeship and obtained a situation in another printing office as an "improver". A supplementary source of income was provided by nightwork at the local newspaper office. The paper was printed by hand on a big, flat press, one side of each sheet at a time, the sheet being laid on the type and the press brought down by hand power. This operation required very

great effort, and the young men who presented themselves on Friday evenings at the newspaper office
invariably retired with a crop of blisters to nurse in
preparation for their next tussle with the printing press.

Enoch was at this time a regular attender at the
Sunday School attached to his parish church. It was
not surprising that a lad who, although inured to
physical hardship, remained emotionally sensitive,
should find in the environment of Sunday School an
escape from the conditions against which he was in
unconscious revolt. Though he was now doing work
not without interest, there was nothing in the manner
in which he earned his daily bread to give him
any sense of achievement. He became a teacher in
the Sunday School. The attractiveness of becoming
a foreign missionary presented itself to him with
increasing force, while the idea of joining the Army
was often present in his mind. Both were roads of
escape, both presented possibilities of adventure and
personal domination.

But it was to less spectacular methods that he
eventually resorted. The boy's work at the Sunday
School and his earnestness had impressed the vicar of
the parish, the Rev. William Beresford, and started
a friendship which was to last as long as the clergyman
lived. Another church worker, Mr. J. J. Sykes, the
head master of the Leek Grammar School, also took
an interest in the boy and his aspirations, and between
them these two decided that the best service they could
render him would be to repair some of the serious

defects which the absence of schooling had left in Enoch's formal education. Enoch gave ready assent to their proposals, and with the same eagerness with which he had set out to earn a living eight years before, threw himself into the task of removing the disabilities which his earlier needs had imposed.

The boy made good use of his time, and soon gave evidence that his instructors were to receive the only reward they sought. Such progress was made that before long the pupil was exploring the mysteries of third declension Latin nouns with Mr. Beresford, while the schoolmaster pressed on with mathematics and composition. "Men of little showing," long since at rest—what revered memories do their shades evoke for the man whose life has raised to their labours an abiding monument!

While he thus devoted all the free time he could secure to educational improvement, Enoch still lost no opportunity of adding to the few shillings a week he was earning at the printing office. Both the vicar and the schoolmaster found him odd jobs about their households with a view to relieving his monetary difficulties, while the interest taken by Mr. Beresford in printing established a common bond and made Enoch's services of especial value. The vicar possessed a tiny plant of a few cases of type and a printing press which, operated by a lever forced from an almost horizontal position to the vertical, gave an impression from the face of the type. The vicar used to fly a white flag from the vicarage when he wanted Enoch to call, and Enoch, who passed that way in going to and from work, was always eager to obey the summons. The work they did—most of it was for the church—gave the boy useful practice.

With the greater confidence that came to him as his education advanced, Enoch began to feel that he might install a small printing plant in his own home. The vicar encouraged him in this idea, and even made him a present of his own outfit. The space at his disposal in the small cottage in which he lived with his parents was very limited, and the plant had to be installed in Enoch's bedroom. But this also was a convenience, for Enoch worked at the press far into the night, and it was pleasant to have a bed so close at hand!

Though every inch of the room was pressed into service, the space remained inadequate. So Enoch decided to build a place where he could carry on his work with greater facility. He considered the small garden at the back of the cottage and decided it would do. He laid a wood foundation, and gradually erected a building. It was the work of his own hands, and it pleased him. He regarded with especial pride the foundation he had laid for a small combustion stove, the most ambitious and hazardous undertaking connected with the new premises. This building had entailed a long neglect of his spare-time printing; but when all was finished and he had carried in the plant from his bedroom, and had prolonged the delight of waiting for the perfect moment by arranging and re-arranging it in varying order, his eagerness to resume printing welled up in a tremendous new enthusiasm for the work.

Meantime he was actively engaged in both Sunday School and Band of Hope work. He became local secretary of the Band of Hope. Arranging outings and entertainments for children made a specially deep appeal to him, and as in these affairs the expectations were as large as the funds were small, to accommodate both exigencies called for an ingenuity at improvisation which Enoch's experience well qualified him to provide. Excursions in canal barges, with tea-parties on board, were a treat which the children greatly enjoyed, and many happy holiday afternoons were so passed. The shrill voices of the children rising above the lapping of the water, the plod of the labouring horse and the quiet beauty of the passing countryside are memories still shining brightly when much that was sad and painful is lost in the twilight of the Staffordshire scene.

.   .   .   .   .

It would not at that time have called for any great perspicacity to foresee a successful career in the printing trade for Enoch Hill. He was working hard for his employer and, in his spare time, for himself, and gaining a reputation for reliable work. Everything pointed to the probability of his progressing in this trade. Then chance stepped in. Enoch, in short, fell in love. And as a result of this twice-happy circumstance all Enoch's pushing energy and resourcefulness were directed into the service of the Building Society movement.

Like Enoch himself, Miss Esther Haynes was an active worker in the parish of St. Luke. She and Enoch were frequently meeting in the Sunday School and in work at the mission church, and the friendship based on this community of interests soon grew into a deeper attachment. Esther was an orphan, living with her uncle, and Enoch became a frequent visitor at their house. The uncle was completely blind, but he was a clever and successful accountant, and in spite of his handicap was secretary of the Leek United Building Society, which was expanding steadily under his guidance. He found his niece's suitor—not then twenty years of age—an interesting and promising young man, and devoted many evenings to helping him in his efforts at education. Hill in return used to read to the blind man.

The Building Society movement, one may pause to observe, was still in an amorphous condition. In the beginning it was essentially a working-class thrift enterprise, directed in particular to the acquisition by its subscribers of the houses in which they lived or desired to live. Early in the Industrial Revolution, when high rents were being charged to workers crowding in from the rural districts, the idea grew that the rent system was a costly mistake. The money which was being paid merely for the loan of a house might equally well serve to buy it and, the house once bought, no further rent would need to be paid. The fear that in consequence of a strike or unemployment there might be no money for rent, and therefore no home,

3

would be removed. At a rent of £12 a year, or less than five shillings a week, a tenant would at the end of 10 years have paid £120—or, if allowance were made for compound interest at the rate of 4½ per cent, £150. This sum would be more than the value of most of the cottages in which workers lived; and, having paid it, the tenants would have something a great deal better to show than a collection of rent receipts.

How long the problem in this form was pondered there is no record to show, but eventually the solution was found in the formation of clubs for the purchase of houses. A subscription was fixed, the same for each member, and building was begun on a block of houses the number of which was determined by the membership of the club. As soon as the first house was completed, lots were drawn and the fortunate member moved in, this procedure being repeated until every member had procured a house. By this time the last subscription had been received and all the houses paid for, and the club was wound up. To Birmingham belongs the credit for having established the first Building Society, or at least the first of which any record exists.

Although these Building Societies were affected to some extent by the Friendly Societies Act of 1829, it was not till seven years later that the first direct legislative effort to regulate their activities was made, in the form of an Act for the Regulation of Benefit Building Societies. This Act, which referred to the

societies as being established principally among the
"industrious" classes, was passed some ten years
before the first Permanent Society was formed, but
fortunately for the movement there was nothing in it
to prevent the extension of the idea to embrace this
wider form of thrift.

The next step was the formation of what were called
Terminating Societies. Instead of houses being directly
purchased by the societies, loans were granted which
enabled the borrower to exercise some freedom of
choice as to the kind of house he purchased. But as
the societies had no resources other than those sub-
scribed by the members, who themselves required a
loan as soon as they could get it, the system of balloting
had to be retained, and inevitably it led to abuses,
including the sale of allocations.

Finally, about the middle of the century, the "permanent" principle was evolved. It sprang from a
recognition of the existence of a growing class of people
practising thrift on a small scale, for whose resources,
amounting in the aggregate to a considerable sum, no
attractive outlet existed, for the savings banks paid
low rates of interest. The stocking and the teapot,
indeed, continued in popularity with these people, for
there at least savings might be kept in tangible form,
while the sacrifice of interest was almost negligible.
Between this class and the people who desired to buy
houses there was of course no strict line of demarcation.
But there could be no doubt of the existence of large
numbers who were saving with no intention other

than to provide for old age or possible sickness, while many others were anxious to purchase their houses without being able to afford more than a part of their earnings each week.

What could be more reasonable than to "match" these two sets of people—those who wanted immediate cash for a house and were prepared while living in the house to pay interest on the money instead of rent for the house, and those who for a longer or shorter period simply wanted to save and get interest on their money? Could not the complementary interests of house purchasers and investors be served through one organisation? If so, it should comprehend the best of all bargains, for both sides would benefit.

The first Society to put this idea into practice was established at Chelmsford in 1845. The ascription "permanent" arose from the circumstance that a continuous inflow and outflow of funds was maintained and it was thus no longer necessary to wind up when the members had finally paid for their houses. To this new kind of society a ready welcome was accorded. With its wider appeal to the thrifty, the movement gained increasing resources and purposiveness. Social workers and various religious denominations banded together for the formation of societies, and it came as a new discovery to an increasing number of people that instead of paying rent for the profit of a landlord they could transform the money into interest and purchase instalments for the benefit of themselves.

Equally revealing to others was the discovery that a good rate of interest could be earned, not only on large sums of money but on small amounts saved from week to week—and secured, moreover, on bricks and mortar. Small wonder that the movement spread rapidly, until there was scarcely a town of any size in England that did not possess at least one Society, or a branch of a Society established elsewhere.

Its track was not, of course, without casualties, although the movement went strongly ahead. While the soundness of its principles had been fully established, and were eventually to be justified to an extent far in excess of the most sanguine dreams of those who first formulated them, they were not always applied in a business-like or even, on occasion, an upright manner. Where difficulties occurred, they were to be found almost invariably among small societies established by well-meaning but, quite often, ignorant men, drawn from the class which the societies were designed to help. They were in consequence unable to give the supervision that the work required, and unable also, from lack of resources, to employ a skilled staff that would have supplied their deficiencies. The officials who were appointed sometimes proved fraudulent, but most of the catastrophes that occurred were due less to actual dishonesty than to the absence of a proper audit, which would have taken account of such questions as that of proper allowance for depreciation of property which had come into possession and interest payments that had fallen into arrear. The conduct of all the larger societies was above reproach, but the occasional lapses of their lesser brethren had a retarding influence on their work. A Building Societies' Protection Association—the forerunner of the Building Societies' Association—was formed in 1869, with the principal object of promoting legislation for the regulating of building society activities. A Committee of Inquiry was appointed in 1872, and the Act of 1874 followed.

This Act permitted societies to become registered and incorporated and thus able to execute deeds by the fixing of the corporate seal, and to hold property under power of foreclosure without the intervention of trustees—a privilege removing the cumbersome restrictions which had hampered the societies in dealing with loans on property that had fallen hopelessly into arrear. The societies were also enabled to receive money on deposit from non-members.

Most of the existing societies took advantage of the Act and became incorporated. Business continued to expand, but the movement continued to produce its crop of irregularities, and it was not till the Act of 1894, with the stringent audit and statutory form of accounts it imposed, that the movement can be said to have obtained the order and security that the best and by far the preponderating elements within it desired.

But widespread as was the recognition thus accorded to the value of the principles of mutuality and permanency as applied to the financing of home-owner-ship, the movement, even half a century after the developments which had given it such new impetus, remained a small thing for small people. Its greatness lay all ahead. When the time came, it would be ready.

And when the time came, so would Enoch Hill.

CHAPTER III

EARLY DAYS AT THE BUILDING SOCIETY

NEVER at any stage of its career did the Building Society movement appear to represent a protest against the existing economic order. Its reliance on individual effort corresponded too closely to the spirit of the nineteenth century to attract the support of the rebellious. It did not hold up the capitalist class as enemies of the "dispossessed", but rather said in effect, "Go and do likewise." Ownership was enthroned. Hence the emotional fervour which springs from righting real or imaginary wrongs was absent, although the movement was not without a proselytising zeal of its own. Many societies were in fact established by local worthies and careerists whose intentions were amiable enough but whose thoughts ran in directions quite different from the founding of New Jerusalems.

This philosophy of economic regeneration by individual effort was, long before he had formulated it even to himself, a guiding force to Enoch Hill. Suffering had evoked in him neither resignation nor rebellion, but simply an active desire to seek a remedy. The desire for social reform has been traced to the competition of childhood for the favour of the parents and to the consequent early development of the sense of justice and injustice in the distribution of desirable things. Whatever validity this theory possesses, it finds at least negative confirmation in the absence from the mind of Hill of any sense of grievance against society, and a corresponding absence of the need for "mothering", for almost as soon as he had learned to do anything for himself, he had found someone a degree more helpless calling for assistance. As the eldest of the family he had assumed towards his younger brothers and sisters a parental rather than a competitive role, and self-reliance, learnt as it was in the formative years, became a habit with him. It was emotionally, if not physically, effortless, so that when long years of unremitting toil produced but scant result, his faith was not submitted to any questioning. For him, to go on trying was just to go on living.

Hill was twenty years of age when the Leek Building Society claimed him as a very junior assistant. He and Miss Haynes had been lovers for eighteen months, and Hill had grown increasingly into the favour of her uncle, the Leek Society's secretary. The work of the Leek Society was steadily expanding, and when further clerical assistance was required a small position was offered to Hill.

The office of the Society chanced to be in a room adjoining the general office of Leek County Court, and the clerk to the County Court was the brother of the Building Society's secretary, and his chief assistant. It was the practice of the Building Society's assistants and the County Court staff to render each other clerical aid in busy times, and through this arrangement Hill gained a useful insight into County Court work.

Hill continued to run his private printing business after he joined the Building Society, and even so still found his energies unexhausted. It was his ambition to open a bookseller and stationer's shop, and with the assistance of Mr. John Robinson, a Deputy Lieutenant of the County and a lay reader at the church, this desire was fulfilled. Moreover, Hill taught himself shorthand, and, having acquired a useful degree of proficiency in this art at a time when it was much less widely practised than it is to-day, applied for a post, and obtained it, as representative for the north of the county of the *Staffordshire Advertiser*, the county newspaper printed at Stafford.

These were laborious days, and if Hill did not forsake delights, it was only because he had never indulged in any. His duties at the Building Society occupied a normal working day. In addition, he rose in the early hours of the morning to collect huge parcels of papers and periodicals from the station, shouldered these to his shop, and proceeded to put things in order for the day. Then to the office at nine. His printing work was done at meal times and in the evenings, and his reporting work in his spare time.

Busy as was his working life, the claims of the Church were not put aside. He was admitted a licensed lay reader of the Diocese of Lichfield in 1887. In Hill's parish of St. Luke the vicar and one curate were responsible not only for the parish church services but also for the services in two mission churches, at the Union Workhouse Chapel and at the Cottage Hospital.

There was therefore considerable scope for lay readers, and Hill not infrequently found himself with as many as three services to take on a Sunday. It is recorded that in one mission church some three miles from his home at Leek, Hill conducted evening services on over one hundred occasions. Fortunately he was a good walker; the churches were long distances apart and there was no other means of locomotion. From time to time he assisted single-handed clergymen in remote parishes in the country, duties that often involved walking twenty miles in the course of the day.

Setting off from Leek one Sunday morning to walk to a mission church twelve miles distant, coatless as was his wont, he was overtaken by torrential rain. He sought shelter and the loan of a coat or umbrella at the house of a small farmer with whom he was acquainted. The farmer welcomed him warmly, and pressed him to stay until the family broth, preparing in a pot over the fire, should be ready; but the farmer had reluctantly to admit that he had neither coat nor umbrella to lend. Under the stimulation of the broth he did, however, remember that an old overcoat was enjoying retirement from active service in the cowhouse. With some pride of discovery he unearthed it. Alas! It proved to have so many colours and so many holes that the missioner feared his appearance in it at church might create a prejudice, and decided to proceed without it.

Another week-end took him into the High Peak district, which was difficult of access, there being no railway and no other method of conveyance within his means. He walked on a Saturday afternoon to the town of Longnor, ten miles away, and as he had promised to take three services on the following day to enable the vicar to take a holiday, he was given a bed at the vicarage. His first duty on the Sunday morning was to take a service at a chapel three miles away. He invited the company of the village shoemaker and gossip, a man with artistic and especially musical leanings who had been organist at Longnor Church until, many years before, some difference of opinion had arisen between the vicar and him. The shoemaker had not been in the church for years when he went this Sunday morning. Hill knew his friend's vein of humour, and, looking him in the face as he gave his address, illustrated his theme, that the practice of religion did not necessarily mean damping down all innocent pastimes, by telling the story of the merchant who advertised for a porter. To a young man who applied the merchant put a series of questions:

"Are you a total abstainer?"

"Yes."

"Do you gamble? Do you smoke? Do you attend football matches?"

"No."

"Do you attend cricket matches?"

"Sir," said the applicant, "I understood you advertised for a porter. It is an archangel you want."

As the preacher had expected, the shoemaker chuckled prodigiously. Indeed, his amusement was so clearly expressed that the gravity of the preacher himself through the rest of the service was only precariously maintained.

But lay reader's work was usually more arduous than humorous. Hill on one occasion walked three miles in deep snow to take a service at the mission church, only to find at the end of his difficult journey that the only person in the church was the cleaner. He put on his cassock and surplice, however. Then he asked the cleaner if he would like the service to be conducted. The cleaner said he would, and Hill thereupon read the service and preached his sermon to the audience of one.

Strenuous as were some parts of his lay reader's work, it was in the service of the County Court that perhaps the most exhausting day of his life was spent.

One Monday morning, when the bailiff officials of the County Court should have made journeys into the hilly country in the neighbourhood of Buxton, two separate bailiffs returned to the office with the report that owing to the depth of the snow, which had been falling heavily for some days, it would be impossible for them to reach some dozen outlying hamlets ten to fifteen miles from Leek. It was the last day on which the various processes could be served to be returnable for hearing at the next court, and when at noon the second bailiff brought back the papers, the Registrar's anxiety that the business should be ready for the judge's consideration at the next court was so plain that Hill volunteered to make the journey.

He started just as the mills were discharging their workers for the midday meal. Longnor, ten miles away over very hilly exposed country, deep in snow, was his first place of call. To get to it he had to push and struggle through snowdrifts which in many places were higher than his head. He was so completely wet through when he reached Longnor that he had to accept the loan of trousers and stockings from a friendly man at one of his houses of call. From Longnor he walked three miles along the road towards Buxton for another call; then back to Longnor; two miles out again in the direction of Bakewell; back to Longnor; four miles out on the Ashbourne side; then two miles farther to another hamlet on the Derbyshire side. By the time he had distributed all the documents it was late at night and all the inns were closed. He was therefore faced with a walk of ten miles home over a bleak moor, along a road which was almost obscured by deep snow and had no hedges or buildings to mark it.

Somehow he managed to find his way, half-walking, half-feeling, through the darkness and snow until he arrived home, in an exhausted condition, in the early morning. He had walked forty miles in deep snow.

For this effort he received the reward of six shillings, but the County Court officials had been impressed by the performance, and for years Enoch Hill's walk was pointed out to the regular process-servers as a proof that no task they were given was unreasonable.

Hill married Miss Haynes in September, 1887. He

was then drawing a salary from the Building Society of thirty-nine pounds a year. This was small payment, even for those days; and the low salary tradition is one from which the movement has never completely emancipated itself. This sum, however, by no means represented the whole of the newly married couple's income, for it was supplemented by the young man's outside activities. Even so, it was no more than sufficient to cover the upkeep of a very modest dwelling. The house in which they began married life was similar to that in which Enoch had been brought up. It consisted of an entrance lobby, a small sitting-room, a kitchen, and two bedrooms, and the rent was four shillings and sixpence a week. As soon as he had scraped together enough capital to cover the difference between the cost of a house and what the Building Society would lend upon it, he bought a house of his own; but it was some years before the Hills reached this happy position.

CHAPTER IV

REACHING UPWARD

IT is not surprising that the sitting-room in the Hill's first establishment should have quickly lost its character and been transformed into a workshop. After his marriage the small printing plant which Enoch had erected at his parents' home was transferred to the sitting-room of the new house, where, having acquired a treadle platen printing machine, he was able to enlarge the scope of his work. Hill now turned out the parish magazine and a variety of circulars, cards and small posters. But business was not plentiful, and on one occasion at least only his tenacity of purpose prevented the printing enterprise from receiving an abrupt check.

Hill had obtained an order to print the quarterly statement of accounts of the local Co-operative Society, which ran to several pages. He did not possess the suitable type, but in the expectation that regular orders would follow the first commission he bought the type, although its cost, to him, was high. Then after the first issue he was told by the officials that future work was to be executed elsewhere.

The type he had bought was suitable for no other purpose, and the threatened loss was severe. He requested an interview with the directors, but was repeatedly refused. He kept on asking, however, and

48

his persistence at length won him the interview. He explained to the directors the problem presented to him by the sudden withdrawal of their patronage, and he gained, not only their sympathy, but, what was more important, the repetition of the order.

About this time Hill tasted beer for the first time— not by design, but by accident.

He had learned that an auction sale of printer's plant, including some type which he wanted, was to take place at Birmingham, and he travelled the sixty miles distance by train to attend the sale. It was late in the evening before the lot in which he was interested was put up for sale, and he had no time to get a meal before catching his train from Birmingham to Stoke-on-Trent *en route* for Leek. He did not reach Stoke till after eleven o'clock, and then he found that there was no train to Leek that night, neither was there any refreshment-room open, and his purse was inadequate to the cost of staying at an hotel. He therefore set out to walk the twelve miles to Leek.

As he trudged along the stirrings of hunger, "sharper than the sword", became insistent. Passing a cottage by the roadside in a colliery district, he noticed a lighted room on the ground floor. He went up the little garden path and knocked, once and again. At his third knock the door was opened slightly and a face covered with coal-dust peered through the crevice. Hill explained his predicament and asked for a drink of water. The man indoors replied, "We have no water and my wife is ill," and shut the door. The importunate traveller knocked again, however, and the collier reopening the door, said, "I told you we have no water. You can have a drink of ale if you like." He offered a tin can containing ale, and the traveller drank deeply and gratefully.

Hill also allowed his part-time employment to invade the little general living-room of his home. Here he fixed a second-hand kitchen dresser, which had the form of a long table containing nests of drawers for household use, and a flat surface for work. At this he and his wife made by hand hundreds of thousands of paper bags, orders having previously been secured from shopkeepers by canvassing. The bags were sometimes plain and sometimes had tradesmen's advertisements printed upon them. It was very thinly paid work, comparable to some extent with the re-muneration of a match-maker; but no contribution, however small, to the family exchequer was despised, and the work, if strenuous, was happily performed. His wife was a wonderful helpmate, bright and cheerful through all the efforts to win success.

In this little home their first child was born, in October, 1888, but, to the sorrow of his parents, lived only three days. A second son, John Henry, was born in November in the following year. He is now the head of a firm of solicitors with offices in Halifax and London. This son was educated at Denstone College, Staffordshire, one of the chain of Woodward schools, where he earned an enviable reputation as an athlete, winning distinction as Rugby footballer, swimmer and boxer. He played for his college in many important matches, and was the college representative in boxing contests against other public schools, some French schools and British Army teams. The Sports Instructor at the college acclaimed him with pride the best man he had trained in the use of the gloves.

After some years the Hills' home was transferred to the shop premises he had acquired in Leek for his bookselling and stationery business, and an upper room was equipped, as in his former house, as a small printing office. Here he employed his three brothers, and, with his many duties and undertakings, it was no unusual thing for him, and for his wife, to crowd sixteen or eighteen hours of labour into a working day.

His newspaper work at this period led to an interesting, if rather worrying, experience. For a number of years he had been reporting the news of the district for the *Staffordshire Advertiser*, and had refrained from taking any side in political affairs. One evening he set off on his cycle for a village a few miles distant to report the proceedings of a meeting held on behalf of the Liberal candidate of the day. The meeting was not well attended, and the candidate announced that he would not make a formal speech, but would express his views upon political matters generally, and afterwards answer any questions addressed to him.

He referred to a proposal to disestablish the Church of England, and stated, as an example, that the disestablishment of the Church in Ireland was approved by every person of influence in the land. No questions were submitted, but Hill, who was interested in the question upon religious grounds, asked the speaker if he could name any influential public man in Ireland who had expressed such approval, as from his recent reading he had gathered that the reverse was the case. The Lord Archbishop of Armagh, he pointed out, had recently stated that the disestablishment of the Church in Ireland had been nothing but an evil, with no compensating advantages whatever. The candidate had no direct answer to this question, which was followed by other questions from the audience, and in the end, when a motion to express confidence in the candidate was proposed and seconded, it was defeated on a vote.

On the following afternoon, at a largely attended meeting held at the Leek Town Hall and addressed by a well-known and influential Member of Parliament from London, Hill was severely lectured upon the wickedness of newspaper reporters intervening in politics. For some time afterwards he was troubled by a nervous fear that what he had done quite innocently might imperil his position, humble as it was, in the service of the newspaper.

Every little item of income was important in those days. His remuneration as a reporter was on a somewhat fickle and uncertain basis, being at the rate of one penny for every line printed by the newspaper, and no reward was paid for reports crowded out, and only a proportionate payment for reports abbreviated. As these lines were printed in nonpareil type, exceedingly small, the lines, eagerly counted at the week-ends, appeared few in number compared with the time and labour expended in attending meetings and writing up reports. Other work of various kinds was sought and found—he had a collection of little shopkeepers whose accounts books he kept written up; he collected accounts owing and rents for a small commission; and he cultivated, with some success, agencies for insurance companies.

His youthful habit of leadership in his humble home no doubt unconsciously governed his business policy, because, in the course of time, all his three brothers and his father became associated with him as assistants in his various business pursuits. Failing health prevented his father from carrying on the heavy work of a manual silk twister, and he became assistant to his son as a commercial traveller in connection with the printing and stationery business.

Enoch's interest in sport extended to both cricket and football, which he played whenever an opportunity presented itself, although this was not often. But if change of work is true relaxation, he no doubt derived considerable benefit from the variety of his occupations. Newspaper work had aroused his interest not only in political but also in educational affairs, and particularly in technical education. But when the Education Committee of the Leek Urban District Council co-opted him as a member to represent the printing trade, a trade union storm broke upon his head.

Letters appeared in the local Press pointing out that Mr. Hill had not been an indentured apprentice to the

trade and consequently was not a fully fledged journey-
man printer, and the local Union of Printers formally
protested to the Council against the appointment.
As Hill determined not to be ousted from the Committee and from the work in which he was so keenly
interested, he accepted this opposition as a challenge.
He gained the consent of Sir Philip Magnus, who
was Chairman of the City and Guilds Technical
Educational Union, to present himself for a forth-
coming examination at the Technical School, Manchester, in practical and theoretical typography, and
sat with a large number of trained students. Then
he proceeded to the practical test given at the printing
works of the Co-operative Society. He passed with
high marks, although forty per cent of the trained
students failed! And he returned to his work for
technical education with the voice of criticism
stilled.

There is no doubt that Hill felt attracted towards
journalism as a profession, and it might have claimed
him but for the chance that created another kind of
place that he was particularly qualified to fill. As it
was, he found time amid his many pursuits to complete
a *History of the Ancient Parish of Alstonefield*, and to
write a number of local guides, including those to
Alton Towers, Leek and Rudyard.

The combination of efforts had its natural result,
and in 1895 he suffered a partial breakdown in health
which compelled him to relinquish his clerkship at
the Building Society and look to his business activities

to provide him with a living. In the following year, however, the secretary of the Leek United Building Society died suddenly, and the directors offered to Hill, on the condition that he should devote substantially the whole of his time to the office, the position of secretary and manager. This involved the sacrifice of a good deal of valuable work and the foundation of a successful business, but he felt that in the interests of his health it would be prudent to curtail his responsibilities and devote himself principally to one job. Consequently he accepted the appointment in 1896. This made it necessary for him to dispose of the book-selling and stationery business, and at the same time he transferred to his father and brothers the printing business, which they afterwards conducted separately, with his supervision and assistance so far as that was compatible with his new position.

To enable the printing business to have the advantage of extended plant it was removed to new premises, and the capital available from the sale of the book-selling business was largely expended on machinery and power for printing. Hill and his brothers co-operated in the purchase of the *Leek Post* newspaper and a limited liability company was formed, of which Enoch became Life Governor. He has been continuously associated with the production of that journal during the thirty-seven years which have passed since. The newly formed company purchased the first linotype setting machine to be put down in the north of Staffordshire, and as the linotype is one of the most complicated mechanisms in existence, and there was no experienced man in the neighbourhood, Hill set himself the task of mastering the intricacies of the machine. This demanded long spells of work through the night until the staff of the paper were able to handle the machine themselves.

He was at this period elected a member of the Leek Urban District Council, and served upon various committees, including the Finance Committee and the Gas Committee. If in those days there had been any housing activities, Hill would have been deeply interested in them, because his work as manager of the Leek United Building Society brought him into close contact with housing problems. He was fully conversant with and concerned about the exceedingly unsatisfactory conditions of and facilities afforded by the houses which were available on a rental basis to members of the working classes. His home life, as a child and youth, was spent in three houses which contained the very minimum of accommodation and comfort, and in not one of these was there any bath or hot water, and in two of them there was no internal supply of cold water. It was not, in fact, till he himself had reached middle age that he enjoyed the comfort of a bathroom in his own house, having previously had to resort to public baths.

Hill had never believed that the property being offered by landlords to their tenants constituted the best houses possible at the rents demanded. He felt that much could be done to increase the home comfort even of those who were unable to go in for home-ownership through Building Society facilities. His views were shared by Mr. James Cornes and the late Mr. James Adams of Leek, and the three co-operated in the erection of a large number of good houses of much improved design, with modern arrangements, baths, etc., although Hill had no financial interest in the scheme. These houses had patent fire ranges by which one fire was provided for two rooms, and supplied hot water for domestic purposes—an arrangement which since has been widely adopted.

Upon his appointment as manager of the Building Society his salary was arranged to include all necessary clerical assistance, and he took into his office his youngest brother, a likeable, tall, good-looking youth. The boy was attracted, however, to a sailor's life and was determined to go to sea. His ambition was strongly opposed by his father, and it was only after realising that if the boy did not go to sea with his consent he would go without it, that the father was prevailed upon to withdraw his opposition. Hill then decided to make the best of the circumstances, and paid a premium to a firm of Liverpool shipowners, and provided his young brother with an outfit as an inden-tured apprentice upon a three-masted sailing barque, registered at Liverpool, then lying at Hamburg and bound for San Francisco. He took the boy to Hamburg to join his ship and left him there, with a return ticket and money in his pocket to bring him back home if he should change his mind.

Then followed a harrowing series of events. Three months later his father died, no doubt partly from grief, and in less than three months again Hill learned that his brother, owing to the breaking of a ratline, had fallen to his death from the mizen-top of the barque when nearing San Francisco and been buried at sea. The father and son had been greatly attached, and neither knew of the death of the other. It was a sad day for Enoch Hill when he had to tell his mother that her affliction and sorrow had been doubled, and that her dear youngest boy had been lost.

CHAPTER V

AT HALIFAX

BETWEEN his appointment as manager of the
Leek United Building Society in 1896 and his depar-
ture in 1903, Hill brought up the Society's assets
from £51,000 to £103,000. His thoroughness was
again manifest in his determination to acquire the
highest professional credentials for his work, and soon
after he took up full-time duty in charge of the Building
Society, he became an Associate of the Chartered
Institute of Secretaries. He was later appointed a
Fellow and Member of the Governing Council of
the Institute, and in 1933 was chosen as the Institute's
treasurer. The Society at Leek having made such
rapid progress in his hands, the directors were well
satisfied with their choice, while in the town itself
Hill was being regarded with increasing respect.

At the end of 1902 the secretaryship of the Halifax
Permanent Building Society became vacant. This
Society was one of the largest in the country, and the
position was widely advertised. Three hundred applications for it were eventually received, one from
Enoch Hill amongst them. His chance did not look
particularly bright. He was entirely unknown to
anyone connected with the Society or even living
in Halifax. In fact, he had never been in Yorkshire in
his life.

59

That his application survived the competition with many influential names was perhaps due to the originality with which he presented it. He prepared an attractive brochure in which were printed a copy of his application and copies of his testimonials, and one of these booklets he presented to every director of the Society. This enterprise must have aroused the directors' curiosity, for they sent a deputation to Leek to see Hill and consider the local conditions.

He was invited, with three other selected candidates, to attend at Halifax a meeting of the full board. On the day of the interview his turn to go into the board-room came last. An old official of the Society who was present recalls that after Hill had been interviewed there was no further doubt. The voting in his favour was unanimous. As there is no reason to suspect that the board were possessed of more than a normal amount of prescience, it must be assumed that Hill's ability was strikingly apparent.

Although the Halifax Building Society had been established for fifty years when Enoch Hill became its chief executive officer, he was only the second to fill the post of secretary, the first, Jonas Dearnley Taylor, having been the prime mover in the formation of the Society. Taylor, a solicitor's clerk, had in December, 1852, when he was only twenty-four years of age, called together a meeting of local business men and put before them a project he had conceived for the establishment of a Building Society. Although the "permanent" principle had recently been adopted and the movement was spreading in many places, the idea still held all the elements of novelty. Taylor had thus to explain his proposal in some detail. The support of John Fisher, the manager of the Halifax Joint Stock Banking Company, who presided at the meeting, was warmly accorded to Taylor's plan, which the two had previously discussed together. This, with Taylor's enthusiasm, carried the meeting, which agreed that a society should be formed.

The project was well received when approaches were made to people prominent in the life of the town. Among the patrons were the Member of Parliament for the Borough and the Mayor.

The Society began business on February 4, 1853, in an upstairs room in Old Market, Halifax. The rules which had been drawn up and incorporated in a barrister's certificate provided that meetings to receive subscriptions were to take place every Friday evening at 7 p.m. The directors would attend in rotation, their remuneration for this service to be sixpence for the first half hour and one shilling for the second. If they failed to attend they were to be fined two shillings. Stewards were to be appointed regularly by members of the Society, and they were to receive sixpence for each night they attended.

The Society was well patronised from the beginning. The regulations were simple and attractive. The shares were valued at £120 each and were divisible into fifth parts of £24 each. On one share, 2s. 6d. was payable weekly or 10s. per lunar month. The rate of interest allowed was 5 per cent compound, at which the full value of the share—£120—would be reached in thirteen years seven months. For borrowers, shares were valued at £60, and the amount of the loan was reckoned as so many shares of £60 each. Tables were provided showing how the shares, including interest, would be repaid in small weekly or monthly instalments.

In April of the Society's first year a prospectus was circulated in which it was stated:

"The promoters would earnestly beg the working classes to examine carefully the claims this Society has upon them: for the appropriation of a fifth part of a share brings the Society within the reach of all, there being but few who are unable to subscribe sixpence a week; and as there is no other institution open to take so small a sum and pay interest thereon at 5 per cent, the directors would earnestly desire their co-operation, feeling assured that by so doing they will be fostering a proper habit of saving; and the money thus saved will always be in readiness against bad trade, sickness or death."

The response to this appeal was very large, and shortly afterwards it was decided to open the office daily, with Jonas Taylor in charge. Taylor even advocated the opening of branch offices in outlying districts, such as Sowerby Bridge, Elland and Huddersfield. The directors, taking the view that it was premature to talk of extending before their first year had been completed, were not easily convinced, but Taylor had his way, and the policy of developing business in other towns through the establishment of branches was vigorously pursued.

At the first annual meeting, held in March, 1854, it was announced that the receipts for the first year amounted to £11,333 and that there was a balance in the bank of £1,389. The actual profit for the year was returned at £179.

Progress continued uninterrupted. By the end of nine years the total assets had reached £95,000. By 1865, the first period for members buying their houses reached its conclusion, and a profit of £2 13s. 5d. was declared on each share.

In 1871, a second Halifax Building Society, the Equitable, was formed with an influential backing. The success of the Halifax Permanent Society had been so notable that many who had not participated in the venture were glad enough to join in a project the practicability of which had been so handsomely demonstrated. There were others who thought the new Society would not last long against the formidable competition of the firmly established Halifax Permanent. But the pool of Yorkshire thrift had by no means been drained, and ample resources flowed into the new Society without in any way disturbing the old one, and the two organisations progressed side by side. In 1882 the assets of the Halifax Permanent reached the million mark, and although the same year brought the death of the president, John Fisher, whose support had been Taylor's mainstay from the beginning, the work went on.

The two Halifax Societies were little affected by the Liberator crash of 1892. Although the Liberator was not strictly speaking a building society and quite definitely was not run on building society lines, there was enough resemblance to create a public scare, and in the run on building societies which ensued many societies whose affairs had not been conducted with caution were brought to the ground.

In 1897 the secretary of the Halifax Equitable died, and was succeeded by Harger Mitchell, a man of considerable energy whose efforts still further increased the Society's business. In 1898 Mitchell suggested to the directors that a small bank should be opened in connection with the Society. Although progress was continuing favourably, a certain number of accounts were being lost because of the Society's inability to issue cheque-books. Mitchell could not, however, point to any precedent, so that his recommendation was not immediately adopted; but eventually the board were persuaded of the reasonableness of the proposal, and a bank began business on January 1, 1900.

The most cautious regulations were adopted. Building Society members alone could hold shares; no overdrafts were allowed; and only those who kept a minimum credit balance of fifty pounds were allowed the use of a cheque-book. Business grew steadily, and after six years a dividend of $7\frac{1}{2}$ per cent was being paid. But still greater progress lay ahead.

The Halifax Permanent Society by 1902 had reached its jubilee year, and Jonas Taylor was still secretary. But in September of that year he passed away, and when, early in 1903, the meeting which celebrated the completion of fifty years' work was held, the destiny of the Society had passed into the hands of Enoch Hill.

.   .   .   .   .

Hill went to Halifax with an anxious heart. His wife, who had been ailing for some years, was obviously not recovering her health, and soon after their arrival at Halifax she fell into a painful illness which was to end a year later only with her death. This first year was thus one in which new and greater responsibilities had to be borne, together with deep personal sorrow. Mrs. Hill remained cheerful until the end, and her courage did much to ease the double strain on her husband. After her death, however, and after his son had returned to school, Hill began to feel that he was really alone, a stranger in a strange place. His domestic life, for the next few years, was drab and monotonous.

In 1906 Hill married again, his bride being Miss Bertha Henrietta Byrom Gee, the daughter of an old Leek friend, Mr. Samuel Gee, a distinguished musician and organist. In those early days at Halifax, and constantly, as his duties and responsibilities increased, the present Lady Hill gave her husband a charming and sustaining companionship.

Before his second marriage Hill bought the house at

Halifax—Willow Hall—which has been his home ever since. It is an unpretentious but ancient manor-house, an excellent example of early seventeenth-century domestic architecture which remains much as it was three hundred years ago, except that the façade has been altered and the interior arrangements modernised.

Having bought the house, Hill had inscribed above the lintel of one of the inner doors the legend "East, west, Home's best"—a happy commentary upon the purchaser's life-work, which has since established so many homes both east and west in the land.

Despite the distraction of trouble and grief at home, Hill spared no effort in his work, and the Society went forward in a remarkable manner. By 1906 the Halifax Permanent had become the largest building society in the kingdom, with assets in excess of one and a half million sterling. Of the publicity value of this achievement Hill was fully aware.

At that date the possibilities of advertising were but dimly realised. Such advertising as was done by building societies was mainly confined to an occasional few lines in the local Press. Directors were inclined to look askance at any expenditure on publicity, which did not seem to bring any contra credit. But Hill appreciated then the truth that others took time to learn, and when, shortly after his arrival at Halifax, an official informed him rather nervously that the quarter's expenditure on advertising had reached a total of £1,000, his reply was "Go ahead." The Society's position as "the biggest in the country" was not, therefore, allowed to remain unnoticed, and advertising its success naturally helped to make the Society grow bigger still. It is interesting to note that the example in advertising set by the Halifax Permanent was soon followed by others of the more progressive societies.

In 1908 the directors invited the building societies of the United Kingdom to hold their annual conference in Halifax, and when the meetings were held there, in June, Hill read a paper entitled "The Building Society Movement and the Borough of Halifax."

He told the delegates how out of the chaos of slum property in the town order was coming through the efforts of the two large Societies operating there with the support of the thrifty members of the working classes who were eager to have well-kept homes of their own and glad to be able to do so on a business-like footing. His address made a great impression, and from this day Hill was recognised as one of the most important younger men within the movement.

A further development, the formation of the Halifax and District Permanent Banking Company, followed in the succeeding year, as the result of repeated requests by members and depositors of the Building Society, who wanted facilities for withdrawals by cheque. The development also met the competition for occasional savings which would collectively form a valuable part of the Society's funds. Hill, actively supported by the directors, set himself to the task of establishing this bank, which, although formed as an independent institution, carried on its business at the head office of the Building Society in Princess Street.

The business of the Halifax Perfect Thrift Building Society was transferred to the Halifax Permanent in 1910. The "Perfect Thrift" was a small but sound concern, and all the mortgages taken over showed a good margin of security.

By this time the Halifax had gone far ahead of any other Society. It had 6,000 more shareholders than any other Society, and the total number of accounts exceeded 30,000. It also enjoyed the advantage of having its securities spread over a wide area, with the consequence that the spread of trade depression in one district would affect only a small percentage of the whole.

The next advance was to introduce the "Home Bank" system, which in later years was widely adopted by thrift and banking institutions. Little steel safes were lent by the Permanent Bank to its depositors, who placed their odd coins in them and periodically took the safes to the bank to have the amount saved entered to their credit. The attraction of this method lay in its "painlessness", as odd sixpences were never missed when pushed into the safe, and "mounted up" in a surprising and delightful manner. During the first year 950 of these little safes were issued.

At this time Hill was using his influence in the direction of granting mortgages on smaller properties, for he felt strongly that the true function of the movement was not merely to lend money on good security, but to lend it where it would serve the greatest good of the greatest number. At the Society's annual meeting in 1911 he stressed the desirability of smaller mortgages in larger numbers.

"It is interesting to compare," he said, "the years 1903 and 1911. In 1903 our holding of small mortgages was only 15 per cent of our total; this year it has increased to 38 per cent. Yet, satisfactory as this increase is, it should be greater still if we are to fulfil our real object as a mutual benefit society."

Read in the light of recent Building Society history, when the small mortgage has become the mainstay of the movement and every Society, which can, boasts of its high percentage of small borrowers, these observations show the sureness of Hill's touch and his genius for Building Society work.

By the next year the Society's assets reached almost £3,000,000, and in 1913—the sixtieth year of the Society's existence—exceeded that figure. The Halifax Society was then able proudly to announce itself as "the biggest in the world!"

Hill was by this time an increasingly active public figure in the town, and in 1913 was appointed a magistrate for the borough. In the same year a notable compliment was paid to the Halifax Society by the American building societies. The president of the Halifax Society, Mr. Thomas Whiteley, and the secretary were invited to attend the annual conference of the American societies at Milwaukee, Wisconsin. The invitation was accepted. But within a month of the date on which he had arranged to sail from England, Hill was struck down by appendicitis and had to undergo a severe operation. He was determined, however, to go, and go he did, while still convalescent. He was somewhat limp when he arrived after the voyage, and grew more so when he found himself in the midst of an August heat-wave. But the conference was highly successful and useful. From it grew the International Congress of Building Societies, and Hill was appointed secretary of the first congress, which was held in London in the following year.

And then came the war, with its profound consequences to the Building Society movement.

CHAPTER VI

THE WAR AND AFTER

ONE of the best years on record was reported at the annual general meeting of the Halifax Building Society in March, 1914, and nothing but continued progress appeared to lie ahead. Five months later war was declared and the future which had seemed so assured was—what? To the spirit which the Building Society represented war was the supreme enemy. What its consequences would be to the system of combined thrift and house-purchasing that had been built up none could say. That the duty of the societies was to support the country with the means at their disposal was agreed, and this they loyally did.

Speaking at the annual meeting of the Halifax Permanent, following the outbreak of war, Mr. Thomas Whiteley, the President, said:

"It may be as well to consider what effect the war has had upon this and similar societies. Coming as it did like a bolt from the blue, totally unexpected by the great majority of the people, and I believe by the Government itself, we were at once plunged into a crisis that seemed serious enough to shake such institutions as ours to their very foundations. Your directors felt at the outset that caution was the watchword, and, although smaller loans were continually granted, for a few months all large loans were refused or deferred. As confidence became gradually restored, however, the work of the Society resumed almost its natural course."

The nervousness of all concerns dealing with money was not without justification. Currency inflation, if carried to extreme lengths, would have completely swept away their foundations. A collapse of currency would have destroyed the value of building society assets, which consist not of houses but of mortgage deeds expressed in terms of money. It is equally true that their liabilities to the shareholders and depositors are expressed in terms of money and that the societies would have had both sides of the accounts similarly affected. But under such conditions their ability to render further service to the cause of home-ownership would have disappeared.

At the end of the first war year the mortgage advances of the Halifax Permanent were only £12,140 smaller than in the previous year. The receipts for the year showed an actual increase. Immediately after the outbreak of the war a circular was addressed to the members of the Society indicating that the directors were prepared to give sympathetic considerations to the position of any investing or borrowing member who was unable to pay his subscription for the time being. In a number of cases relief was granted. But though it had been deemed prudent to hold a large sum of liquid resources to provide for any emergency that might arise—the balance at the bank was increased from £189,327 to £318,416—the total withdrawals from all departments amounted to only £573,105, or £48,379 less than in the preceding year. Current receipts were well in excess of these withdrawals, so the Society's resources were never subjected to any strain.

When, in 1915, the Government called for the second War Loan, every facility was given by the Society to allow immediate withdrawals by investors who desired to lend their money to the State, the usual notices of withdrawal being waived. The amounts withdrawn were in consequence abnormally large, but in spite of this depletion of the Society's resources the Society found it possible to subscribe directly a further £80,000 towards the loan. The year 1915–16 saw an increase in the ordinary business of the Society of £249,000, rates of interest paid to investors having been adjusted to the level dictated by those ruling on gilt-edged securities.

In those strenuous days Enoch Hill's skill and capacity for sustained work were among the Society's greatest assets, and the directors were not slow to recognise that in him they possessed a tower of strength. At the annual meeting in March, 1916, Hill was invited to join the board of directors as managing director. Alderman Brear, who had been a director for twenty-three years, had recently died, and it was to the position on the board thus rendered vacant that Hill succeeded.

During 1916–17 the sum of £441,000 was lent to

the Government, and business continued to expand, the year's income increasing by £41,564. Over one and a half million pounds' worth of advances had been applied for, but the actual amount lent was only £540,191. The Savings Bank was also going briskly ahead and the number of "home safes" now in use was no fewer than 8,735.

The appeal for the third War Loan, in 1917, found the Society in a still stronger position, and as a lead to the country the Society made a direct subscription of £200,000, and members followed by investing a further £400,000. Later in the year a further £120,000 was so advanced. But the Society was like the widow's cruse, and its funds could not be depleted. At the end of the year during which these huge sums were advanced the liquid funds amounted to £923,650, or £160,371 more than in the previous year.

But this rapid growth of the Society's business coincident with the expansion of the bank's activities created a problem of office accommodation that by 1917 could no longer be deferred. Either the banking business must be moved into a separate building or it must be sold. The question of disposing of the bank had been raised by the approaches of several of the larger banks who desired to absorb this thriving business. While the matter of office accommodation was under discussion, a handsome offer for the bank was received from the Union Bank of Manchester, and this it was decided to accept. The terms provided a large premium for the bank's shareholders. Hill had been managing director of the bank from its inception, and after the transfer he was appointed liquidator. By liquidating the bank he had founded and managed, Hill, it is believed, performed a function unique in the history of banking. On the transfer of the business to the Union Bank, Hill was appointed chairman of the Yorkshire Board of the bank, a position he has held ever since.

During the war period the Society's assets increased by nearly £6,000,000, and nearly £1,800,000 was lent to the Government, while on the books were over 68,000 open accounts. With the staff depleted by war service—forty-one members of the staff were so engaged —the responsibilities of management and the determination of policy amid the unprecedented financial conditions placed a heavy strain on Hill. In addition he was invited to co-operate with the Government in matters connected with rent restriction, the raising of loans and the insurance of property against enemy air-raids. Once again his capacity for sustained effort enabled him to undertake each fresh duty as it came, even though his normal building society work had increased almost beyond measure.

It was recognised that when the war ended there would be a great demand for houses, though the extent and instability of the demand had not been fully gauged. What was in fact experienced was the full force of the drying up of speculative building for some years prior to the war and the virtual cessation of house building during the war. Building in the pre-war years had been checked by the new land taxes imposed in the Budget of 1909, by the tendency for costs to increase and by the increasing demands made upon property owners by local authorities, who were very properly insisting upon the observance of a higher standard of sanitation and construction. Property as an investment thus began to lose some of its appeal. The rent restrictions imposed during the war, and maintained in some degree ever since, prevented the development of a rent ramp in its worst excesses, but as it kept rents from rising to a level which would have been dictated by the free play of supply and demand, private enterprise in the construction of new houses to let was put out of action.

To buy or to build was the choice confronting those who, when the war was over, were faced with the necessity of obtaining a house. Building costs and property values were prohibitive, but in the first fine careless rapture of peace and heavy Government disbursements, prices were scarcely questioned. That the nation would shortly be in the grip of organised deflation was not foreseen, nor, in the absence of any popular interest in monetary affairs, such as was to come in later years, would its significance have been recognised in any case. For the building societies a new public was created, and borrowers flocked to their doors. And against the fall that was to come in property values the societies had two bulwarks—the operation of the redemption principle, now rigidly insisted on in the granting of loans, and the choice they were able to make from the large number of applications that came forward for loans.

Though the principle of granting subsidies to stimulate the construction of small houses was not adopted by the Government until the end of 1919, it had in fact been recommended by Hill during the war period. Had his advice been accepted when it was first offered, before the great advance in building costs had taken place, a great economy would have been effected, not only because the subsidy required per house would have been considerably less, but also because building development would have been more evenly spread and part of the advance in prices of materials obviated. Hill was eventually to become a keen critic of housing subsidies, on the ground that under conditions of full employment of labour and capital in the building industry their effect was merely to put up costs, and that frequently the subsidies were secured by people of comfortable means whom it was quite unnecessary for the community to subsidise.

So far, £110,000,000 has been spent on housing subsidies, and a million houses erected with their aid. The issue is one which thirteen years' experience has not resolved, and to which, therefore, we must return later.

At the end of 1914 the total assets of the building societies amounted to £66,000,000. By 1918 the figure was £68,500,000. But the exigencies of the war years had wrought a marked change in the composition of the assets, mortgages having decreased by £8,000,000, and other investments—chiefly War Loans—increased by £10,000,000. The societies were thus possessed of large liquid resources available for use in their normal business. In 1919 nearly £16,000,000 were lent for the purchase of houses—twice the amount so lent in 1914.

Not only among would-be house-owners did the building societies find a new public. The Government's War Loan operations had created a new class of investors, and here the building societies found a new source of capital. With the standard rate of tax six shillings in the pound, the attractiveness of the building society shares, interest on which was paid free of tax, required no demonstration. And as the functions of building societies and the very real nature of the security they had to offer became better known, this investment support expanded. Although nearly £16,000,000 was advanced in 1919 and £25,000,000 in 1920, funds not employed in mortgages remained practically unchanged, so great was the inflow of new investment money.

Had not the building societies been ready with their resources and organisation to attract the nation's earnings, and canalise them in the direction of house purchase and construction, the range and scale of the housing activities of post-war Governments would perforce have had to be immensely increased, with what effects and with what success none can say. Since the war, a million houses have been built with building society aid, and the spirit of home-ownership has gone through the land. To this stabilising force must be attributed much of the resistance which the nation has shown to the disintegrating effects of unemployment, truly described as the greatest of social solvents.

·　　·　　　·　　　·　　　·

Following this brief and inadequate account of the contribution of the Building Society movement to a solution of the post-war housing problem, we must turn to consider the predominant part played by the Halifax Society, or, more accurately, the two Halifax Societies, the Permanent and the Equitable, which Hill was eventually to bring together as the Halifax Building Society.

As soon as the war was over a rush of applications for loans was received by the Halifax Permanent; and with large sums awaiting investment at their disposal, the directors were able to grant all applications where acceptable security was offered. By 1920 loans were being granted at the rate of nearly £3,000,000 a year.

But the rapid growth of the business had by this time again caused congestion in the office accommodation, despite the sale of the banking business. The offices which the Society had acquired in 1873 would, it was thought, be adequate for all probable developments, and part of the upper premises had been let off. Now the whole of the building was occupied by the Building Society; and still more room was needed. In consequence, York Buildings, a substantial block of property in Commercial Street, was purchased, and after reconstruction was ready for occupation in 1921.

When the Society moved into its new premises assets had reached £9,345,000, and the number of open accounts exceeded 100,000. Thereafter the tale of growth proceeded unchecked towards the astronomical figures of recent years. By 1923 the assets had reached nearly £14,000,000 and the income £10,000,000.

The Society now held in its vaults more mortgages than there were dwelling-houses in the borough of Halifax, had more open accounts on its books than the number of the entire population, and held assets four times greater than the total indebtedness of the town.

But even in 1923 it was realised by Hill that real as the progress was in the provision of houses for the thrifty, not more than the fringe of the slum problem had been touched by the subsidised efforts of the local authorities. At the Society's annual meeting in that year he referred to the number of people with small investments in building societies who should be encouraged to buy houses of their own. To the thrift motive should, in brief, be added the home-owning motive:

"We should get these people moving up out of houses they now occupy, owned by somebody else, into houses which they have provided for themselves, and so make room for someone to follow them from below. There would be a general tendency upwards, and it would eventually empty the slums. We must work from the top, and although it has not been popular I am perfectly satisfied that it was good statesmanship that we should get control of the expensive houses first, because they are occupied by the people who have the means to do something for themselves."

Upon this "filtering up" process the National Government ten years later are still placing some reliance, though it is doubtful if the older houses which through this process become available are the most suitable for slum emigrants.

The activities of the Halifax Permanent were now nation-wide. A large office was taken in Charing Cross Road, London, in 1924, to facilitate the direction of business in the south of the country. By 1926 a thousand new accounts were being opened every week with the Society, and at the end of the following year the total number of accounts had reached 221,162. The Society had been in existence seventy-five years, and no less a sum than £146,000,000 had passed through its books. Not one penny of this had been lost, and there had never been delay in payment on withdrawals, or failure to pay an attractive rate of interest.

Side by side with the progress of the Halifax Permanent, the Halifax Equitable Building Society had been making headway in almost as remarkable a manner. The two Halifax Societies were by far the largest in the kingdom. The assets of the Equitable in 1921 had reached £3,000,000, or more than double the figure of three years previously, while by 1924 the total had become £7,000,000. In the three succeeding years assets increased at an average rate of £2,000,000 a year.

That these two great institutions operating in Halifax should eventually become one seemed inevitable, and in 1927 negotiations for union were opened and finally effected on January 31, 1928. There were 75,000 mortgages in the Permanent and 40,000 in the Equitable, but the whole of the property became vested in the new Society in a single deed. When the amalgamation was first publicly announced Enoch Hill said:

"The union between the two Societies is a perfectly natural one, and it gives the opportunity to the two institutions as corporate bodies to put into practice the gospel of thrift which they represent and preach to the individual. In addition to the greatly added financial strength which will be the immediate result of the combination of the two Societies—which is shown by the fact that the total reserve funds will exceed one million pounds—there will be from the outset a very considerable degree of economy. The benefit in this respect will not be merely immediate but constantly increasing, and this, of course, will be for the benefit of the members and depositors of the united Societies.

"There are other important considerations also, because a union will consolidate and concentrate all the building society influence and sentiment, at

82

present associated with both Societies, into one, and the sound and well-proved commercial principle upon which both Societies have been working for some years may become the pattern and standard of similar societies not only in England but throughout the English-speaking world."

In preparation for the amalgamation and the transfer of the Equitable Society's business to the offices of the Permanent Society, extensions to the Commercial Street premises were undertaken, and completed by December, 1927. So enlarged, the offices covered an island site in the main thoroughfare of the town. They were opened on December 2nd by the late Lord Birkenhead, then Secretary of State for India.

Of the new Society, Hill became President. It was reported in March, 1928, that the combined assets resulting from the merging of the two Societies were £46,981,482. This figure comprised the amount due on 97,567 mortgages, securities, bank deposits and office premises. The total number of subscribers was 329,224. The gross profit, after payment of all expenses except interest to shareholders and depositors, was £1,828,621, while after meeting such interest there was a surplus of £359,457. The reserve fund totalled £1,461,200.

Such was the account of his trusteeship which Enoch Hill rendered after twenty-five years at Halifax.

CHAPTER VII

ACHIEVEMENT

HOW the widening influence exercised by the Halifax Permanent Society during the war brought Enoch Hill into consultation with the Government on matters connected with housing and national financial policy has already been told. The post-war period which witnessed a spectacular growth of his own Society corresponded with ever-increasing demands upon his time on behalf of the movement generally, which, operating on an undreamed of scale, was now assuming a new significance in the life of the nation.

Hill had been elected a member of the National Association of Building Societies in 1914. At the annual conference of the association at Bristol in 1921 he was elected chairman, and he held that position uninterruptedly for twelve years. It was the period during which the movement leaped to the forefront with almost breath-taking speed. Year after year new records were created, and progress continued at a pace which industrial depression seemed powerless to decelerate. Such rapid expansion naturally brought with it many problems for the solution of which there were few precedents. Hill stood at the helm, taking his ship through an uncharted sea, and, though the passage was not free from storms and alarums, made the harbour and resigned his captaincy without so

much as a scratch on the paint! Once again his
capacity for sustained work and imagination served
him, and the movement, well.

In 1925 H. F. Cellarious and Senator Hennesey,
leaders of the Building Society movement in America,
came to Halifax to invite Enoch Hill, as chairman of
the National Association, to visit the United States
and preside at the International and Centenary Congress of Building Societies to be held in Philadelphia
in 1931. The invitation was accepted, and to the
memorable visit that followed we shall refer again in
a later chapter.

The contact which Hill established with Government affairs during the war increased the interest in
politics which his early newspaper work had roused.
It was inevitable, because of his vigorous independence
of mind, that his sympathies should lie with the
Conservative Party, although with the "die-hard"
element within it he had little in common. Above all
else in his political philosophy he placed the improvement of the conditions of the working classes, with
whose sufferings under the unrestricted private enterprise of the nineteenth century he was only too well
acquainted. But he believed that in their amelioration
self-help had still the predominant part to play, and
that the exercise of this function provided the spiritual
and physical foundations for a useful and contented
life. Individualism had been his lifelong creed, but
combined always with a broad humanism—individual
effort for the common good.

Between 1922 and 1929 Hill stood for Parliament in the Conservative interest in four elections, but was defeated on each occasion. In the constituencies he contested he was fighting a forlorn cause, and with little other prospect than to improve the voting strength of the party, which he did. He went to his home town of Leek, in 1922, to oppose the sitting Socialist member, a trade union official in the division. He was defeated, but returned the following year for the 1923 election, in which he was defeated again. At the request of the Conservative organisation he stood for Huddersfield in 1924, and, although unsuccessful, increased the Conservative vote to a record for the constituency. He returned to Huddersfield for the 1929 election, and although there was a swing of public opinion against the Conservative Party after five years of Conservative Government, again increased the Conservative vote.

In the election of 1931 he received no fewer than seven official invitations from as many divisions to be the Conservative candidate. He declined them all, however, as his responsibilities as chairman of the Building Societies' Association and president of the Halifax Society—the membership and finance of which had now assumed immense proportions—were now making so great a demand upon his time and energy that he felt unable to undertake active political work. In each one of the divisions he was invited to contest, the cause he supported was successful.

But though he no longer entertains thoughts of

entering Parliament, Hill continues to give active support to the Conservative Party. He has been for many years president of the Leek Conservative Association and, for the past four years, chairman of the Halifax Conservative Association.

Among the public offices Hill has held is the chairmanship of the Advisory Committee constituted by the Lord Chancellor to recommend nominees for appointment on the Commission of the Peace for the Borough of Halifax. Lady Hill was appointed a Justice of the Peace in 1933.

Hill became, also, in 1929, advisory director at the head office of Barclays Bank, Ltd., having been a member of the Leeds Local Board of this bank since 1924.

His connection with the Insurance world dates back as far as 1904, when he was appointed a director of the Yorkshire and Derbyshire Board of the Alliance Assurance Company. He became chairman of that board in 1924, and still continues to fill the position.

The great social value of Enoch Hill's work was recognised by His Majesty the King, and a knighthood was conferred upon him among the Birthday Honours of 1928.

Of the congratulations he received on this occasion, none was more welcome to him than that of his aged mother, his debt to whom he had acknowledged with unfailing devotion and love throughout the years of his advancement.

With his mother he had ever maintained the closest intimacy. When she was not on one of her frequent visits to his house, he rang her up on the telephone every night to exchange affectionate greetings and enquiries. Among the countless Press photographs that have appeared representing Sir Enoch engaged in some public function, the one he treasures most shows his mother and himself at the annual conference of the Building Societies' Association at Buxton. And when the Halifax Society opened an office at Stoke-on-Trent, Sir Enoch had pride in taking the directors and others from Halifax to see his mother at her home in Leek, where she was living with her son-in-law and daughter, Mr. and Mrs. Beresford.

This wonderful old lady lived to enter her eighty-fifth year; her death, when it came in 1931, was a heavy blow to her son.

This deep attachment to his mother is only one—although perhaps the most significant—indication of the fine loyalty rooted in Enoch Hill's nature. Friends of earlier and humbler days are still his well-remembered friends, and his relations with them are maintained with all the freedom of the past.

On receiving the honour of knighthood, Sir Enoch was presented by his colleagues on the board of the Halifax Building Society with his portrait painted by Mr. Richard Jack, and with a replica which hangs in the Society's head office. The Mayor of Halifax presided at the dinner at which these were presented to him, and on this occasion Sir Enoch was happily accompanied by his mother and sister, as well as by Lady Hill and his son.

Although, as he himself admits, Sir Enoch's chief hobby has been "work", he has found time to be a playing member of various golf clubs and to become proficient in amateur photography and fishing. He is a keen motorist, too, and in the course of his business has travelled far and frequently by motor, without the assistance of a chauffeur. In some fifteen years, from 1916, he kept a record of having travelled by road over 100,000 miles in the United Kingdom. He has visited nearly every town in England and Wales, as well as having made numerous journeys to Scotland and Ireland, and his foreign travel, to which we shall later have occasion to refer, has included many visits to France, Belgium, Germany, Italy, Switzerland, Spain, Greece, Turkey, Egypt, Northern Africa, the United States, Canada and Mexico.

His favourite pastime? Let him answer the question in his own words.

"The books I most enjoy reading and the writers who have most impressed me cover a very wide range. You will understand that my opportunities for concentrated book reading are not very numerous or prolonged. I can, however, unhesitatingly say that Charles Dickens's books have given me the greatest pleasure in my life, and I have read most of them a number of times. I am particularly interested in books of travel and biography. I have for many

years taken particular pleasure in reading books
by local authors, and I think I have read everything written by the Brontës, Halliwell Sutcliffe,
Cutliffe Hyne and all books of local interest. I
have also a great regard for Arnold Bennett's books,
am fond of detective stories, and often seek ease
of mind by indulgence in modern novels, of which,
on the average, I read something like two a week.
This, with a regular examination of daily newspapers, pretty completely fills the time I have for
reading.

"I think my favourite form of recreation is golf,
because it takes me into the open air, generally
amongst pleasant surroundings and in genial company, and it affords opportunities for physical
exercise, and at the same time calls for the exercise
of self-control and patience. The real advantages of
golf can be enjoyed in the recreation of walking, but
there is not so much pleasure in walking as in golf.
Golf, therefore, may be said to be a luxurious form
of walking."

The Halifax Golf Club, which Sir Enoch cap-
tained for a few years, is situated on the slopes of the
Pennines and considered to be one of the finest courses
in the country. He set himself the task of restor-
ing its popularity, and succeeded so well that after
three years the club was able to carry through an
extensive plan for improvements to the links and the
club-house.

It was while returning from golf one evening that Sir Enoch was credited with the possession of economical habits far in excess of those to which he may lay claim. The time was just after the formation of the National Government. Economy was in the air—and the Press. Sir Enoch had played his round, pipe in mouth, and had in consequence consumed a little tobacco and a lot of matches. Having a proper respect for the fairway, he tucked the spent matches back in the box. When leaving the club-house at the end of his game Sir Enoch was approached by a burly tramp.

"Oblige me with a match, guv'nor?"

"Certainly," replied Sir Enoch; but on opening his box he found it contained more spent matches than "live" ones, and proceeded to search the box. The tramp watched these preliminaries with unconcealed repugnance, and then with an ejaculated "Well, I'm damned, thrift!" went, matchless, on his way.

To describe Sir Enoch as a "friendly man" is almost impossible without conjuring up memories of Dick Swiveller's reiterated question, yet it is difficult to find a better description of Sir Enoch's attitude towards his fellow-men. And this general friendliness wells up from a deep capacity for personal friendship. No friend or even business acquaintance of Sir Enoch has ever felt neglected; each is made to feel that he "counts", and each does in fact count, for to Sir Enoch the claims of friendship are of equal seriousness with, and worth taking as much trouble about as the claims of business. The ramifications and extent of Sir Enoch's business activities place him among the most fully occupied men in the country, yet no letter or enquiry, however trifling, from one with whom he has come personally into contact but is immediately and personally dealt with.

By this aspect of Sir Enoch's character one business friend finds himself particularly attracted:

"To many of us who meet him in business and in sport it is a constant source of wonder how he remembers and finds time to attend to so many people's interests. He may be at the other end of the country and come across something which he knows will interest one of his friends. Despite his preoccupations he will find time to send a letter the same night. These little attentions and kindnesses mean a good deal. It is flattering to one's self-esteem that so busy a man can remember one's particular interests.

"A small but perhaps not insignificant point is that Sir Enoch rarely arrives alone at the golf course. He always brings a friend or two, or finds someone who would like a 'lift' in his car. Over a period of twenty years I have known of no single instance in which it could be said that Sir Enoch had wounded a fellow-creature's feelings. But there are scores who will tell you with pride of his thoughtfulness for them."

The value of the public services rendered by Sir Enoch can scarcely fail to secure proper appraisement,

but the smaller circle who come into personal contact
with him find

> That best portion of a good man's life
> His little nameless unremembered acts
> Of kindness and of love.

Visitors of all classes and creeds find their way to
Willow Hall, and all carry away with them a memory of
the unostentatious charm of their hostess. But it is not
only in the domestic circle that Sir Enoch finds his
wife so faithful an ally. During his many absences
from home he is kept *au courant* with his personal
business affairs by dispatches from Lady Hill—and
they are written in shorthand.

The influence of a home in which music was an
absorbing interest implanted a love of music in Lady
Hill which the efflux of time has served only to foster.
But this affection, she confesses regretfully, is not
shared by her husband. In her not inconsiderable
library, modern fiction is well represented, but by what
is styled the "realism" of the modern novel she is not
attracted. "It's quite out of date, I know," she says,
"but I do like a novel to tell a story and not read like
an extract from a psychologist's case-book." Her
interest in the form of the novel is partly personal, for
her sister, the late Miss Annie L. Gee, wrote novels
and stories for young people which are still running
into fresh editions.

Like her husband, Lady Hill has lifelong associations
with the Church of England, and one sad memory is
of a life dedicated to Christian service. Her only

brother, the Rev. Ernest Alfred Gee, became a missionary and went out to Central Africa, where he died of blackwater fever contracted while nursing a friend suffering from the disease.

Although Sir Enoch is no longer a total abstainer—if you are at Willow Hall and ask him, he will point smilingly to an exquisite spirit canteen presented to him by the staff of the Halifax Building Society—he finds more stimulation in work than in alcohol, and both Lady Hill and himself are supporters of the temperance movement.

Lady Hill tells of one temperance meeting they attended to which a local vicar, prevented at the last minute from coming to preside, sent his curate to deputise for him. The curate was a nervous young man, anxious to define his exact attitude towards alcohol, and, rising, he explained that he himself was not altogether a teetotaller. Sensing the rather depressing effect of this declaration upon his audience, he plunged on, to become more circumstantial. While it was true, he said, that he could not claim to be a teetotaller he only had a drink of anything alcoholic occasionally—in fact, only when he went to the vicarage on Sunday nights.

.   .   .   .   .

Further extensions to the Halifax Society's head office were carried out in 1931, and the largest deeds' strong-room in the world was constructed under an imposing concert hall, later to be opened as the

"Alexandra Hall" and described as the most beautiful and perfectly equipped little theatre in the country. In it Sir Enoch, as chairman of the "Alexandra Hall" Company, takes no small pride.

The strong-room itself has been described as "one of the wonder spots of the world". The *Yorkshire Evening Post* published a long article on the hidden treasure in Halifax, and we can do no better than quote from it:

"In Halifax's £100,000,000 crypt a dozen men and youths are at work these days. The annual audit of the 170,000 deeds held by the Halifax Building Society has begun. Officials of three firms of auditors—two Halifax firms and one from London —have descended into England's biggest 'hidey-hole' of deeds, where they will remain for about five months. The job is growing bigger every year. One foresees the time when the auditors will not come up at all.

"And the vaults themselves—what is to happen to them? They keep on growing. Only recently the third great extension to them was opened. It looks like the lower deck of a liner, save that it is floored with concrete, and it extends underneath the area occupied by the Alexandra Hall. The ceiling of this gigantic vault is a mass of pipes and ducts, and has fans to carry off impurities and keep the auditors supplied with fresh air. They do say that down there it is almost like being in Blackpool.

But I, for one, would not accept this particular auditor's certificate.

"'There is probably no place in this country,' says Mr. Frank Emmett, the General Secretary, 'where so much value in the form of deeds is gathered together in one place.' For the Halifax is the world's biggest.

"Every single one of the 170,000—and more—sets of deeds has to be actually seen and certified. They are all in numerical order in their boxes, and so complete is the system that if No. 19,579, or No. 1, or No. 169,999 were to be called for by the manager, it could be produced inside a couple of minutes.

"There is a continuous outward and inward flow of documents—outward when borrowers have paid off their mortgages, inward when new loans are contracted, but the inward flow is always much greater than the outward.

"The process of inspection is rapid and thorough. Youths in overalls keep passing to and fro with batches of deeds, which pass before the auditor one by one; are examined by him and passed on to other youths who march off with them to their appropriate lockers. Just over a thousand sets of documents a day are inspected.

"Snags that occur, the Securities Manager, Mr. H. E. Rendell, says, are when a borrower lives, say, in Huddersfield, has property in Harrogate, but pays his instalments through an agent in Leeds. The deeds are arranged in towns, and this may at times mean searching through all three towns to locate a particular document, but they are always found and checked.

"There is romance in those big vaults and those enormous stacks of deeds, for every deed there means a house or houses—nearly every one of them means a home. He who holds the deed possesses, for the time, the property. If four people are allowed as the average number in the families affected by those deeds, it follows that if all these houses and these people could be gathered together they would form two cities the size of Bradford and Leeds.

"Fire is a dread enemy of the hundred-million crypt, and, of course, fire is carefully guarded against. You may not smoke in the crypt, and when the auditors leave in the evenings, the doors are barred, and the place is patrolled all night long.

"But no burglar need think of entering the crypt as a good 'lay'. There is no money there. What is in one sense the richest spot on earth has not a penny piece in it."

·   ·   ·   ·   ·

The negotiations with the Government for a revision of the building societies' income tax arrangements, conducted by Sir Enoch in 1932, are of more than technical significance. The ability of the societies to offer "free of tax" interest to depositors and investors was unquestionably one of the great attractions which drew funds to the movement. Without this facility, the immense contribution to the solution of the housing problem made by building societies in the post-war period would not have been possible. The low rates of income tax prevailing before the war did not render the "free of tax" investment unusually attractive, while during the war, when income tax was rising rapidly, the demands of the Government for loans at successively increasing yields to the investor drew the nation's savings in that direction. But after the war, while income tax remained at the heights to which it had been pushed, and attractive and safe outlets for savings were no longer "on tap", the existence of a safe investment offering a tax-free yield of from $3\frac{1}{2}$ to 5 per cent made an irresistible appeal.

This "tax free" concession is worth explaining in some detail, as it is frequently confused with "tax free" dividends paid by industrial companies. In the latter case the companies have actually paid the tax in full, and the dividend is the net sum after the payment of such tax. Thus, if a company paid a tax-free dividend of 5 per cent, it would in fact be making a distribution of $6\frac{2}{3}$ per cent, taking income tax at the current standard rate of 5s. in the £. This $6\frac{2}{3}$ per cent and not the 5 per cent would represent the recipient's income, so that, if he were not liable to pay tax, he would be entitled to have the difference of $1\frac{2}{3}$ per cent, paid over by the company to the revenue authorities on his behalf, repaid to him.

The building society arrangement is different. It is matterless whether the recipient is liable to pay tax. Upon his building society interest he is not charged, and in no circumstance is he entitled to any repayment of tax.

It might at first glance seem that a "tax free" industrial security is preferable, *ceteris paribus*, to a building society investment. That it is not so is because the price of such securities takes into account the payment of the dividend in this form, and they are thus valued on the basis of the gross yield—the sum of the net interest paid to the shareholder as "tax free" *and* the amount of income tax paid by the company on his behalf.

What *is* true of the building society arrangement is that it does favour the taxpaying investor. Thus the advantage of holding a security the interest upon which is not liable to tax is not apparent in the case of a man whose income is so small or whose family is so large that he would in any case have no tax to pay. He may thereby save himself the trouble of having to make out a claim for repayment; but even this he can accomplish in other ways, notably through the purchase of War Loan. With the investor of more comfortable means, paying tax at 2s. 6d. or 5s. in the pound, the position is very different. A 4 per cent tax-free return is then equal respectively to a $4\frac{4}{7}$ or $5\frac{1}{3}$ per cent yield on which tax has to be paid. It is scarcely surprising, therefore, that building society investments should attract not only the savings of the small and thrifty investor, but also the surplus resources of all classes reaching up to the well-to-do and wealthy.

It was partly in recognition of the increasing number of well-to-do people who were drawing incomes from building societies, and partly because of the exigencies of the financial situation, that the Government decided that the time had come to make a new arrangement with the societies.

It was recognised by the Government that the existing basis of direct assessment on the societies must continue, and interest be allowed to continue to be paid tax free. Any other suggestion would have been met with the strongest resistance. Under the old arrangement, which had been in force for thirty-five years, the societies paid tax at the full rate on the interest credited on all investments or deposits made by corporate bodies and on all sums of £5,000 or over placed by individuals. On the interest on all other deposits or investments tax was borne at half the standard rate on half the amount so credited—in effect the tax was reduced to one-quarter. On the balance or undivided profit tax was charged at one-half the standard rate.

These were undoubtedly favourable terms, and in the protracted negotiations that preceded the determination of a new basis of taxation, the societies recognised that their liability would inevitably be increased. The terms that were eventually agreed upon left the position unchanged with regard to the holdings of corporate bodies and the holdings of £5,000 and over, but interest on all other deposits and investments had to bear a tax at two-fifths of the standard rate. The undivided profit became taxable at the full standard rate.

This arrangement, which involved an increase in the tax borne by many societies of as much as 100 per cent, did not escape criticism, but does not appear to have brought any serious consequences to the finances of any society. After a year's experience of the new arrangement, it was calculated by Sir Enoch, from a sample of twelve societies, that the increased tax paid represented an average increase of interest on the capital employed of .315 per cent, or 6s. 4d. for each £100. But the ability of societies at this period to reduce interest rates paid to investors without affecting the supply of resources undoubtedly mitigated the consequences of the new taxation.

A reference to the opposition to his policy, made by Sir Enoch shortly after the conclusion of these negotiations, brought to him a well-turned compliment. The occasion was the annual luncheon of the Metropolitan Association of Building Societies. Lord Riddell, as President of the Association, was in the chair, and Sir Enoch was the guest of the occasion. In responding to a toast in honour of the association, Sir Enoch remarked that he was in considerable trepidation, as he rather feared that a good many of his friends present would rather have seen his head brought in on a charger like that of John the Baptist. Lord Riddell thereupon rose and said, "If the time ever comes when Sir Enoch Hill's head is brought into the room on a charger, I hope I may be present, because I would like to take the brains."

CHAPTER VIII

AMERICAN SCENE

THE Building Society movement across the Atlantic has not kept pace, relatively to the population, with its expansion in this country. The American's house is not his castle; it is only where he sometimes pauses for rest. Inveterate individualist as he is in public affairs, the American experiences a kind of communistic reaction in private life. While the Englishman entrenches himself in his strip of garden and glowers over the hedge at any eye which would invade his privacy, the public park is good enough for the Westerner; and as for the dining-room—well, is not the snack-bar quick and handy? There are, nevertheless, many large and flourishing building societies in the United States, some of them continuing to operate on the terminating principle.

At the end of July, 1931, Sir Enoch Hill sailed for America to fulfil his promise to preside at the International Centenary Congress of Building Societies to be held at Philadelphia. He led a deputation of 130 representatives from the United Kingdom building societies. Lady Hill accompanied him, and after the congress, the two made a tour of the American continent, and were accorded official receptions in many towns. One of Sir Enoch's speeches was broadcast throughout America.

The letters written home by Sir Enoch, and a diary kept by Lady Hill, provide an interesting record of this tour, and offer many reflections on the American scene. One ceremony at which they were present was the unveiling, in commemoration of the hundredth anniversary of the mortgaging of the first house to a building society, of a tablet on a rough stone or boulder at Frankfort, a suburb of Philadelphia.

"We were all very much impressed," commented Sir Enoch in a letter to a friend, "by the energy and activity of the American citizens and business people. All classes begin work much earlier than we do. Many building societies and other institutions have their staff full speed ahead by 7.30 or 8 o'clock in the morning, compared with 9 or 9.30 o'clock in England. They work tremendously hard. They finish about 5 o'clock or 6 o'clock and have a very short midday interval. . . ."

Lady Hill was interested by the difference between hotels in England and the Canadian ones. Here is one comment entered in her diary:

"The bedrooms here are most delightful—real log huts, made of pine logs put together with plaster on the inside, and very charmingly blended with pitch-pine walls. The lounge is most attractive, with log lampstands and hat racks—in fact, one of the most picturesque rooms I have ever seen. The waitresses, bellboys, chauffeurs, caddies and so on are mostly, if not all, university students working for their fees in their vacations. . . ."

At Toronto, Sir Enoch and Lady Hill were met by a crowd of reporters and Press photographers. It was late in the evening, and the travellers were tired by their journey, but the pressmen were clamorous. There was nothing for it but to supply a "story" and pose in a corner of the station for pictures.

Touring the city next day, Lady Hill's attention was attracted by an immense castle. It had been built by a one-time millionaire named Howard. Every room was panelled, and many of the fittings were of silver. The walk around the castle alone had cost a million dollars, and had been rebuilt three times before the owner was satisfied. The millionaire had shortly afterwards fallen on hard times, and the castle had been seized for rates. It then belonged to Toronto.

That the American business man believes in luxury in the office as well as at home is suggested by Lady Hill's comment on a visit to the office of a friend at San Francisco:

"It is quite a nice office, and his own rooms are really magnificent. He has marvellous cupboards in the panelling for wireless, cigars, coats and all kinds of things. Then he has a bathroom of black marble —a most ornate affair; and on the opposite side a kind of pantry containing all sorts of drinks and dry goods, with glasses and towels and cups and saucers. In the bathroom there are cupboards with dressing-gowns, suits of clothes, and underwear. . . ."

The American's idea of a home seemed equally luxurious.

"One house we visited," wrote Lady Hill at Santa Barbara, "was a gorgeous place, and there were Italian gardens, a Chinese garden in the making and a Japanese one likewise. There were some gorgeous blooms in the latter which the head gardener called 'moonlight flowers'. They were of a heavenly blue, and I should have called them convolvuli. We saw avocados growing—like huge pears, and much used in salads. Italian cypress trees, eucalyptus, banana and palm trees, pepper trees and innumerable other kinds. . . .

"At another rich home there was a park-like piece of ground in front of the house, dotted with beautiful trees. In the music-room were an organ, two grand pianos, a harp and other musical instruments. The gardens were most elaborate, and an attempt was being made to lay them out in various colours—a yellow section, a purple, a blue. The terrace was unique, as it was crossed by a bridge and had seats all around made of huge logs of red wood. The seats had been made by cutting quarters out of tree-trunks. Across the bridge was a tower, from which there was a fine view of the surrounding country and the sea.

"Another notable feature of this wonder-house was a huge stone and marble hall, in the middle of which was a bathing-pool beneath a special sliding roof. Beautiful dressing-rooms encircled it, and this part of the house must have cost a fortune."

The travellers saw films in the making at Los Angeles, where, at the Fox Studios, they met Elissa Landi, Al Jolson and Will Rogers. They saw with amusement that the snow on a "set" in a Russian scene was— mashed potatoes! Later they had a long chat with Douglas Fairbanks, and witnessed the filming of the novel, "Arrowsmith".

One of the actors in this film, Rowland Gowland, recognised Sir Enoch at once, having seen his photograph in the American papers. Ronald Colman was introduced to Sir Enoch and Lady Hill, and they found him as charming in real life as on the screen. They took tea in Mary Pickford's rooms, where they were served by two tall, handsome servants dressed in a livery of white coat, gilt buttons and black trousers.

The suspension of the Gold Standard by the United Kingdom occurred while Sir Enoch was in America. Although traders in this country, and exporters in particular, hailed the decision as a deliverance, the "man in the street" had been led to believe that such a development would be disastrous. The British Government had associated itself with the City attitude towards the Gold Standard, and was generally regarded as prepared to fight to the last ditch for it. After having borrowed £80,000,000 in America and £50,000,000 in France, however, the Government threw in its hand. But its resistance, if not strong enough to suit everybody, was sufficiently marked to suggest that the nation had suffered a financial defeat. It was natural enough that this opinion should be held most widely abroad, and Sir Enoch was called upon to address a number of audiences on the financial position of the United Kingdom. He was able to give first-hand information as to the impregnable strength of British financial institutions, and to demonstrate that the current developments had in no way impaired their position.

The homeward trip was made on the *Aquitania*, and England reached on October 6th. It is characteristic of Sir Enoch that the first thing he did after setting foot in England again was to make for an important business meeting at Halifax.

.   .   .   .   .

At the annual conference of the National Association of Building Societies in 1933, held concurrently with the Fourth International Congress of Building Societies and Kindred Institutions, Sir Enoch announced his resignation from the chair after twelve years' service. "After such a period of service and under conditions so abnormal, particularly during the past two years," he said, "it is very gratifying to reflect that I pass on the responsibility of this great and honourable office not only in a condition of greatly increased strength and influence, but with the scale of operations, funds and membership greatly increased during that period."

The expansion in the movement during Sir Enoch's chairmanship had indeed been remarkable. Membership had increased from 789,052 to 2,560,961 (exclusive of depositors), share and deposit funds from £89,933,615 to £447,634,056, mortgage assets from £75,503,123 to £388,377,535, the total amount advanced upon new mortgages in the year from £19,673,408 to £82,142,116, and reserves from £5,331,659 to £21,699,992.

In the ceremony of according the thanks of the association to Sir Enoch some striking tributes were paid to the work of the man who had "guided our steps through the maze which confronted us". Amid applause it was stated that "he had stood out, above all other men who have served on our executive, in constructive ability, power of organisation, and the vision to see what lies ahead. He has stamped the seal of his personality as fully and completely on the National Association as he has on his own Society, and to-day, right through England, building societies and Sir Enoch Hill are synonymous terms."

After observing that Sir Enoch had been their pioneer, one speaker said:

"I am not making the mistake of thinking Sir Enoch originated the building society movement, but it is safe to say that Sir Enoch, far more than anyone else, remodelled and improved the work so imperfectly begun.

"In its earlier days, the building society movement was a thing of units, of local institutions often controlled by men with very little business experience and small knowledge of finance. The outlook of the societies was very narrow; their policy was merely parochial and their growth was stunted and cramped. It was about this time that Sir Enoch was entrusted with power, and he saw that the whole existing order of things was wrong. He foresaw the great possibilities which lay open to building societies. He saw the need for expansion on sound commercial and business lines, coupled with the highest financial security. He realised that the people must be made to feel without doubt that their savings would be perfectly secure in the building societies. He, sooner than anyone else, saw the greatness of the possibilities which lay dormant but ready for development—the vast expansion in funds and number of members that would follow if only the masses could be roused to a higher social outlook.

"Building societies, as we know, were formed to encourage thrift, and that by thrift their members should become the owners of their homes. Sir Enoch saw how great would be the national asset that could be created by the accumulation of vast wealth in small sums, and he saw that building societies would become one of the most powerful and wealthy institutions in the land, and that their influence would be of untold good to the people. He preached the gospel of thrift and home-ownership;

he advertised this on every possible occasion; he forced it on all the societies and, in time, on the masses; and to him, far more than to anyone else, must be given all the praise for the great success which has attended this movement."

That was in the summer of 1933, and we must turn for a last look at the Halifax Building Society and the position it reached in that year. The annual income was £38,000,000 and the assets totalled nearly £90,000,000. On its books were 530,000 open accounts, and through it 160,000 persons were purchasing their homes. During the year £16,618,000 was advanced to 38,044 new borrowers. And the local institution had carried its message triumphantly into Northern Ireland and Scotland, undeterred by the fact that a Scottish mortgage deed requires to be signed on every one of its seven pages. And then, in the Society's accounts issued in March, 1934, it was shown that the assets had reached £92,642,690, an addition of £3,966,398 on the year. This total represents more than one-sixth of the combined assets of the 1,000 Building Societies operating in the United Kingdom. The net income of the Society during the year was £33,242,525. The amount now due to the Society upon mortgage is £69,607,530, but this huge total is the result not of "big deals" but of the multitude of borrowers which seek the Halifax Society's aid, for the average amount owing on all the Society's mortgage accounts is only £388 each.

CHAPTER IX

CHILDREN'S HOUR

"DURING the long journey of 16,000 miles I have had in the United States, Canada and Mexico during the last four weeks, the children of Leek have often been in my mind, and when I met, as I did in many towns, people who formerly lived in Leek and district, I thought of the stepping-stones that exist, if they can be uncovered, in the old country to bright and successful careers in the new countries of the world."

So wrote Sir Enoch Hill to a friend on his return from the American tour of 1931, and Leek has had ample evidence that Sir Enoch not only often has its children in mind, but holds the uncovering of the "stepping-stones" for their welfare and progress among the dearest of his self-assumed duties. "My young comrades," he has called the children of his native town, and he plans to assist them with the understanding of one who, as he himself has said, "remembers his own boyhood in Leek in similar circumstances to those in which these children are now advancing to their future careers."

One of Sir Enoch's commercial interests itself provided the perfect channel for reaching the maximum number of Leek's young people.

Throughout his life at Halifax he has maintained

unbroken several business associations with Leek, and chief among them stands his joint-ownership of the *Leek Post*. In this journal, early in 1923, a devoted worker among children, Mr. W. A. Smith, began, as "Uncle Nemo", a new feature—"Chats with Little People", which Sir Enoch was quick to perceive offered an unequalled opportunity to get into touch with and help the children of the working classes.

In the past ten years his influence in this connection has become a household word in Leek and district. Thousands of children know his name with affection, and many with gratitude. Some who since the beginning of his work have grown to young manhood and womanhood have written to tell of successes being won which were first made possible by Sir Enoch Hill's provision of "Golden Opportunities". But of these more later.

In the development of the newspaper circulation "war", children's interests have been fairly generally cultivated with disingenuous assiduity. An expeditionary force of newspaper "uncles" and "aunties" has been set on the march, their field-marshal the manager, who knows that behind every child is a potential "registered reader". The *Leek Post* children's feature, however, was started before circulation boosting had achieved this refinement. Beginning with the object of giving encouragement and help where most needed, it has been maintained throughout with that motive unsullied.

Time after time, in letters and in speech, Sir Enoch

has reiterated his own idea of the purpose of the *Leek Post's* children's page.

"It would be impossible to measure or imagine the limits of such work, or the influence it will have upon these young people in their future life, and, I am sure, for their permanent benefit and happiness," he wrote to the devoted originator of the feature; "my pleasurable interest in your great work is due not to its effect upon the *Leek Post* commercially, but to its being an opportunity of contributing in some little way to the happiness and welfare of your 'great-little' family."

At another time he wrote to "Uncle Nemo":

"It has been a real happiness to me to be of any assistance to yourself and the enthusiastic members of your family. I am sure that you are all carrying on work of very real value and usefulness, because not only do you confer pleasure and happiness, but you are really giving a helping hand to my young comrades, who are keenly alive to the advantages of widening their knowledge and endeavouring to understand something of the high level on which human beings may live their lives by self-effort and encouragement. . . ."

His sincerity may be judged by the fact that he was always willing, indeed anxious, to finance joy-bringing schemes for the poor children of the town even when they were not readers of the *Post*. Whenever an appeal to the public was made, Sir Enoch gave a handsome subscription, and was ever willing to provide extra money to ensure that the scheme should be thoroughly carried out and no deserving child missed. His generosity seemed boundless and has been constantly maintained for many years.

Sir Enoch's first expression of interest in the juveniles of the town was in 1923, when he made a grant of five pounds to be offered as holiday prizes through "Chats with Little People". Then came the first of the "Golden Opportunities".

This was a thrilling occasion for sixteen young people. The selected ones were sent to the British Empire Exhibition at Wembley for a week-end, Sir Enoch paying their fares and providing for food and accommodation at the Children's Camp Hostel. The schools in the town had readily agreed to co-operate, for the educational value of the trip was plain, and the lucky children were conducted to the Exhibition by their teachers.

A number of other children who had not qualified for the Wembley visit were thoughtfully given the consolation of a local charabanc trip.

The "Golden Opportunities" were extended in the following year, when, through Sir Enoch's kindness, prizes were offered which included free courses in any subject (with all books and incidental expenses) at a Leek technical school; free courses at the Leek Art School; a violin and free tuition; a year's subscription to the *Children's Newspaper*; and free copies for one year of Mee's *My Magazine*. In addition there were consolation prizes of Savings Certificates and some cash awards.

Children flocked to compete for these prizes, naturally, and Leek began to recognise how keen Sir Enoch was to give its young people a helping hand. Sir Enoch himself was finding a great deal of pleasure and interest in the growing contact with the children, and enjoyed reading their letters and their competition efforts, which were often amusing.

There was the little girl, for instance, who entered a competition of the question "What is your favourite flower?" with a letter that must be as short as any on record. It read:

"DEAR UNCLE NEMO,
 "Violets.
   "Your affectionate niece
        "ELLEN"

On another occasion the children were invited to say why they went to Sunday School. Many of the letters rang ever so slightly false—suggested that the authors were writing what they thought was wanted rather than what they actually felt. But there was authentic sincerity about this one!—

"To get my star-card stamped."

Another quaint effort concluded thus:

"Trusting I have backed a winner,
     "I am,
       "WILFRED
"P.S.—God save Sir Enoch Hill."

An epic excursion to Rhyl—another "Golden Opportunity"—will long be remembered for the way in which a youngster who had got there by false pretences unexpectedly let the cat out of the bag.

Particular trouble had been taken to see that all those included in the party were children who had never seen the sea. Parents and guardians had been required to sign statements to that effect. All seemed well. But as the motor-coach arrived at Rhyl a boy stood up in his seat and surveyed the promenade with a rather critical eye. "Lumme, mister," he remarked, "this place ain't 'alf as nice as what Blackpool is!"

More than one astute little rascal was riding on that excursion, as it happened. On the long journey back from Rhyl competitions were conducted on the buses to keep the children from weariness, and prizes were given. Among other things, the youngsters were invited to tell how they had spent the shillings allowed them as pocket-money. Little Frank stood up and said he had spent a penny on rock for his sister and a penny on a boat for his brother. Mother and father had also been remembered, and there was a balance of sixpence which was to be put into his money-box and saved. This commendable show of generosity and thrift was warmly applauded, and Frank won a prize. Imagine the feelings of the judges when shortly afterwards the bus made a halt and thrifty Frank hurried to a barrow and "banged the saxpence" on ice-cream.

This recalls the distressing disappearance of one, Jack, who arrived at Rhyl with the rest, took his shilling pocket-money, and was told where to report for lunch. After that his whereabouts grew mysterious. No trace of him could be found. But after the police had been co-opted in the search, he was found sitting at a table, patiently awaiting lunch, in the wrong café. But that was not at all the end of the trouble. Jack had purchased a whole shilling's worth of motor-boats at bargain prices (as the motors were broken!) and had left his parcel to be called for. But he could not recollect the name or whereabouts of the shop. No amount of persuasion, not even the offer of another shilling, could move him from Rhyl until the shop had been found. A second search had to be instituted for a shop holding Jack's parcel of broken motor-boats. It was found at length; and perhaps it was not wholly surprising, when you consider what holes a shilling would burn in any boy's pocket, that it proved to be immediately opposite the stopping-place of the bus.

In addition to financing the "Golden Opportunities", Sir Enoch spent a lot of time in helping to plan the competitions. Hundreds of letters on points arising out of the schemes have passed between him and "Uncle Nemo", and Sir Enoch has repeatedly urged that money must not be spared to ensure that no deserving child is excluded, and that every possible opportunity should be used to help the children to realise that they have a place in the world which should be worthily filled. He himself has written many encouraging messages to individual children, besides publishing letters of a similar character in "Chats with Little People".

"I hope you will take the broadest possible view with regard to the admission of as many children as you can, and not risk spoiling the event by excluding any who by the expenditure of a little extra money could be admitted," he wrote regarding a New Year's party. At the same time he wrote to the children, wishing them good health and "great encouragement in your efforts for self-improvement and for the help of each other. I am quite sure that what you are doing will prove of substantial and enduring benefit to you in your future lives."

Sir Enoch's very commendable spirit had the effect that other people began to emulate it. Traders, mill-owners and others supplemented more and more his generous gifts, both by donations and by helping in the organisation of treats, parties, competitions and so on. The influence of Sir Enoch's generosity was felt in hundreds of homes, rich as well as poor, and one admirer, Mr. Robert Schofield Milner, who was himself a benefactor of the town, expressed the view that Sir Enoch's "amazing" encouragement would be proved, in years to come, invaluable.

It was never a mere matter of giving money, admirable and useful as monetary help alone may be. If he saw a chance to help or interest in any way, he would go to great personal trouble. One of the happiest results has been that the children know him as a person and not simply as a name.

Each week prizes were being offered to children on behalf of the proprietors of the *Leek Post*, and, in addition, every now and again came the encouraging gesture from Sir Enoch of a fresh "Golden Opportunity". A monster picnic to Alton Towers, eight or nine miles from Leek, enjoyed by hundreds of children who would otherwise seldom or never have such a holiday, was one of these, although at the time, in 1925, Sir Enoch himself was in ill health and unable to be present. He made a gift of a valuable book to every helper in the scheme as a mark of his appreciation of help given to the children.

In the same year three bicycles were presented through the *Leek Post* to the children; and shortly afterwards Sir Enoch lent the support and publicity of the journal to launch a scheme to install wireless in the Leek Cottage Hospital. He also headed the subscription list with a handsome donation to the fund. Thereafter the history of *Leek Post's* children's corner is punctuated with gifts—of cycles, books and so on; Christmas and New Year parties, summer excursions, cinema treats, and "Golden Opportunities" of various kinds. One Christmas-time Sir Enoch autographed about eighty books for children's gifts; and a wonderful "Golden Opportunity" was that in which children were asked how they would spend a day's holiday if they had not to consider the cost. The prize-winners were given their ideal holiday at Sir Enoch's expense.

The children responded with enthusiastic and loving appreciation. There was no doubting the sincerity behind their fervent huzzahs whenever Sir Enoch and Lady Hill attended any of their gatherings. The Leek Town Hall, at a New Year party given in 1927, echoed to cheering such as had probably never been heard there before, and, indeed, that was an important occasion.

During the proceedings "Uncle Nemo" (Mr. Smith), announced that he had a personal message from the children to deliver to Mr. and Mrs. Hill (as they then were). The children had agreed, he said, that they wanted to give a more practical expression of their appreciation than a verbal vote of thanks, and they now wanted him to offer to Mr. and Mrs. Hill a coffee service and tray as a token of their high esteem and affection.

Two children, Ethel Condliffe and V. V. Smith, came to the platform, removed a covering, and revealed a beautiful coffee service in blue Wilton ware, ornamented with the famous willow-pattern in fine gold. The service was arranged on a kidney-shaped mahogany tray inscribed with the children's message and the date.

The recipient's reply was interesting and characteristic. He spoke at length of his keen desire to foster the education and uplifting of children. No sacrifice that he could make was too great, he said, that would further their mental and moral development and improvement. Anything he had done had been done most willingly, and had brought him a great degree of pleasure. The happy smiling faces before him were his reward.

In a letter written a few days later Mr. Hill referred to the particular appropriateness of the blue and gold willow-ware. It harmonised happily with his home, he wrote, for Willow Hall, which was built in 1610, must have had willow-china under its roof during all the three hundred years since.

The children of Leek were among the first to congratulate Mr. Hill when he received his knighthood. They sent their felicitations at once by telegram, and expressed them more lengthily later through the columns of the *Leek Post*.

It is significant that the schools of Leek have always regarded Sir Enoch's help to the children through the Press medium with approbation. The school authorities and teachers have time and again lent their co-operation, and in at least one school the pupils were allowed to do their *Leek Post* work in school hours, as it was considered a valuable addition to their education.

There is a "Hill Challenge Cup" which goes each year to the child who tries hardest for success throughout the year in the *Leek Post* competitions, and this, as may be imagined, is a great incentive to endeavour. It was characteristic of Sir Enoch's generous way that when he presented the cup, in January, 1930, to its first winner, Maud Owen, he slipped a pound note into it as he handed it to her, "just for luck".

This was another occasion on which the children of Leek made a gift to Sir Enoch. They chose an electric cut-glass table lamp, and many hundreds of children not at all associated with the *Leek Post* were among the subscribers towards it.

A "secret" collecting-box had been installed at a point in the town, and it was a remarkable thing to witness the way in which the children brought in contributions. Some brought silver and some brought halfpennies. One girl contributed a ten-shilling note, saying she felt she owed that to Sir Enoch for the help and pleasure she had had from his generosity. Every class of family was represented in the long file of children who came to express, as their circumstances would permit, their thanks to a much-revered benefactor. The parents also were appreciative, as many grateful letters to the *Leek Post* testify.

The best tributes, however, come from children who have had time to grow up and feel the benefit of Sir Enoch's earlier benefaction. Here are some extracts from typical letters :

"This is my last evening in Leek for some months. On Tuesday I am going to begin teaching in a Council school in Leeds. I have just finished a two-years' course at a training school in London, and heard about a week ago that I had passed my examination. I took drawing for my advanced subject. Perhaps you will remember that many years ago I won a scholarship to the Leek School of Art through your column. I think that was the beginning of my 'artistic career'."

Another former "Nemonite" also wrote to say that, although grown up, she was still feeling the beneficial effects of her early associations with "Chats with Little People". She still retained her certificate of merit along with six other certificates gained later in life.

Then there was the boy who won the first art prize offered by Sir Enoch. He wrote from the Choate School, Wellingford, Connecticut—which is the preparatory school for Yale University, to say that he had become the art editor of the school Year Book.

Numerous other young people, though not already, perhaps, successes in life in the material sense, treasure awards they have had from Sir Enoch, and, indeed, there are few houses in Leek where there are children which do not contain some evidence of Sir Enoch's kindly influence and generosity.

The above letters relate chiefly, as is natural, to the material help Sir Enoch has been able to provide. What is less easy to measure, but probably of greater worth, is the influence of his constant moral encouragement. In the many letters and speeches he has addressed to the children, one observes again and again the urgent wish to impart the secret of successful living as he has learned it from his own experience. "Persistent and consistent striving is the surest road to success," he wrote once in a foreword to some gift books; and he has repeatedly extolled the virtue of "plodding".

A few years ago he was asked by the *Halifax Courier* to write an article on the question "What Chance has Youth To-day?" and the word "chance" was like a spark to tinder. He replied:

"That which has the appearance of a 'stroke of luck' is often the reward of patient, unobtrusive plodding. I like proverbial wisdom, and there is a proverb that says 'Chance is on the side of the prudent'. Chance, in its true significance, must count for nothing; but opportunity must be sought and seized. 'While the shoe is on thy foot, tread on the thorns.'"

And Sir Enoch shares with Henry Ford the view that opportunities are more plentiful for young people to-day than at any previous time. "A generation ago," Henry Ford wrote in his book "To-day and To-morrow," "there were a thousand men to every opportunity; to-day, there are a thousand opportunities for every man." To Enoch Hill it seems that the opportunities which free education and increased leisure time lay open to-day to every youth are "so numerous as to become bewildering". But chief of all, he wrote in his article for the *Halifax Courier*,

"you have the opportunity to strive, the power to

cultivate and develop the natural ability you possess. Seize the small opportunity . . . pursue it diligently and reach out constantly for the greater opportunity that always lies ahead. Success in life is not wholly built on mental ability. The homely virtues of diligence, punctuality, loyalty and enthusiasm—summed up in one word, 'character', still pave the way to promotion and a prosperous career. These . . . are assuredly the stepping-stones to higher things."

And as in Sir Enoch the opportunist is subservient to the idealist, he did not end his answer there.

"Do not overrate worldly success," he added, "but aim rather at the happiness which springs from physical, moral and spiritual health."

CHAPTER X

A HOUSING EXPERIMENT

BUILDING societies are not primarily concerned with housing problems in their sociological aspect. They stand, it is true, for home-ownership and the pride of possession that springs from it, and are sustained by an ardent desire to see more houses and better houses. A remark made by Sir Enoch during a discussion on slum clearance is often quoted. "When I pass through some of our towns," he said, "I feel that a few carefully placed sticks of dynamite would materially improve matters."

But the approach of the building societies to the housing problem has always been individualistic. Their resources are derived from individual thrift, and as trustees for their investors it is their duty to lend only to reliable borrowers. Not the needs of the would-be borrower but his trustworthiness and ability to offer security are the criteria which the societies apply. Had they pursued any other course or adopted any but a strictly business standard, their usefulness would have been limited by their failure to attract the support of investors. Their contribution to the housing problem, immense as it has been, in consequence stopped short when it reached the point of financing the requirements of a class who could not provide a margin of security represented by the difference—some 30 per cent—between the price of a house and what would be lent upon it.

They were sustained in this policy by the maintenance of the demand for loans from a good class of borrower. Though the shortage of houses was, some fourteen years after the end of the war, only felt by the poorer classes, who were in a position neither to take advantage of Building Society facilities nor pay the rent of municipal houses, there was still a steady request for new houses of the £500 to £700 class. Thus the slackening off in the demand for "middle class" property expected to result from extensive building over a number of years, did not occur, and though the economic crisis of 1931 led to a temporary falling off in demand, normal conditions quickly asserted themselves. Calculations made as to the amount of housing shortage to be overtaken had in fact been wrongly based, the total population having been taken as the criterion and the change in the composition of the average family—the unit for which the house is required—neglected.

It is estimated by Sir Raymond Unwin that every thousand of the population to-day require forty-eight more houses than they did in 1911. In Sir Raymond's own words:

"If you multiply the population of 1911 by forty-eight per thousand you will find that it accounts for 1,700,000 more dwellings required to provide for the population of 1911 at the present time than would have given one dwelling for every family in 1911. That is, if not the sole, certainly the main explanation, why the whole of the building we have done since the war has still left us with the war deficiency to make up."

Using the 1931 Census figures, Sir E. D. Simon, in his admirable book, *The Anti-Slum Campaign*, points out that there were 10,233,000 private families and 9,402,000 separate dwellings, giving a shortage of 831,000 houses at that date. No further explanation need be sought for the continued demand for houses. How effectively it was being met at the upper end we have already seen.

It had been recognised for some years that the great need was for small houses to let at a maximum rental of ten shillings a week. Presented in this way, the problem lay outside the scope of the building society movement, which had been built up by its appeal to the thrift and house-ownership motive of the individual. But the movement was fully aware of the existence of a class the needs of which its activities so far had left untouched, and listened sympathetically to proposals having for their object the utilisation of part of the huge resources of the societies for the construction of the smallest class of house. But naturally the societies sought to retain the building society principle of home-ownership in this suggested extension of their work.

When negotiations with the Government were opened at the end of 1931 the building societies put forward a scheme under which the Government would give assistance to individuals to become owners of their own homes on an occupier-borrower basis. The building societies would make abnormally large loans secured by mortgage, and supported by the guarantee of a local authority or the Government, to assist individuals to enter into personal possession and make themselves responsible for the redemption of mortgages by contributions in lieu of rent. At the Annual Conference of the Building Societies' Association, held at Bournemouth, Sir Enoch Hill urged the advantages of this scheme.

" I have for some time past," he said, "given publicity to the idea that the Government, instead of spending millions of pounds per annum in building houses unsuitable for and unattainable by those who are suffering most from the house shortage, could, with economy and success, co-operate with building societies to mobilise the savings and the earnings, especially of young people, for the purchase of their homes by instalments. The principle was established by the Housing Acts, 1923 and 1925, to the limit of 90 per cent of value. If the Government, by its guarantee of safety, would support our mortgages, there could be provided for approved borrowers new small ideal homes of a particular kind, to the number of hundreds of thousands, and the workers in the building industry could be fully employed. The only risk the Government would take would be limited to any deficit which might arise from the negligible proportion of defaulting borrowers, and this cost would be infinitesimal compared with that involved by building houses to let at uneconomic rents.

" This plan would completely solve both the slum and overcrowding problems. That it is practicable has been proved by experience.

" At various periods, in the region of seventy years ago, public-spirited employers of labour in the borough of Halifax arranged with the Halifax Permanent Building Society that, in consideration of the Society's granting mortgage loans to owner-occupiers up to the full cost of artisans' dwellings, such employers would guarantee any deficit which might be realised by the Society in connection with such mortgages. Many hundreds of houses were accordingly built in the town and paid for by the occupiers out of their earnings, with valuable consequences: employment was increased in the building trades, improved homes were acquired by the occupiers, who were thus assisted to save considerable capital, which, in many cases, laid the foundation for successful careers for their children and opened the way for an improved standard of life, and in some cases to independence. The scheme was not only entirely self-supporting—not a penny piece being lost either by the Society or the guarantors— but the benefits of home-ownership were proved and the prestige of the Society established."

But the Government apparently felt that this kind of scheme would not make sufficiently wide appeal to the class whose needs it was devised to meet. There were large numbers to whom the idea of house-purchase was still a novelty, and in consequence to be viewed with suspicion; and probably still more who would be unable to find even the small margin between the building society loan and the cost of the house. Estimates had been prepared to show that the fall in the price of building, together with the cheaper capital available, had rendered the construction of small houses to let an economic proposition and one therefore which private enterprise might tackle.

In consequence the provision of houses to let was kept to the forefront and negotiations to this end were continued. Proposals framed by the Housing Committee of the National Association of Building Societies that the societies should enter, with the aid of guarantees from the Government and the local authorities, into financing the construction of small houses to let at ten shillings per week were favourably received, and in the end the Housing (Financial Provisions) Act of 1933 was drafted. The negotiations were largely conducted by Mr. Walter Harvey of the Burnley Building Society, who has distinguished himself within the movement by his enlightened and well-informed views on housing problems.

It is perhaps too early to pronounce judgment upon the Act, but it has so far exhibited more elements of failure than promise of success. Because of this it has been stated publicly that the societies had not, at any time, promised to work the scheme, but this is quite contrary to the facts. What is true is that the societies, for reasons which will be clear, did not feel that the Act was all that could be desired, but of their intention to support it there is no doubt. Sir Enoch expressed the societies' attitude in his speech to the Annual Conference of 1933:

"The Housing Act (Financial Provisions), 1933, has been the subject of prolonged discussion and consideration between the Ministry of Health and the Housing Committee of the Association under Mr. Harvey's chairmanship, which has done prolonged and useful work. Ultimately the sub-committee, with the authority of the Council, offered its whole-hearted co-operation to the Ministry to give effect to a scheme, the purpose of which was the twofold one of cancelling building subsidies made at the expense of the ratepayer and taxpayer and to provide an adequate supply of modern convenient houses to let at low rentals to a section of the community who have not sufficient means to come within the scope of home-buyers with building society facilities.

"The Act is not in every respect what a great many building society officials—including myself—would have liked, because it makes no provision for assistance to those who desire to become owners and not merely tenants of homes. However, it contains and promises a degree of usefulness which I think entitles it to our hearty support. It is associated with the vital and urgent question of

removing or improving slum dwellings. In my view
the only way to overcome the slum question is to
destroy or immensely to improve the slums. If this
is the most sensible way of tackling the difficulty,
surely a preliminary essential step must be the
provision of suitable houses into which the dwellers
of slums may be transferred. Successive Governments have missed golden opportunities of mobil-
ising all the interested influences in connection with
clearing slum areas by retaining the confiscatory
principles of Section 46 of the Housing Act,
1925.

"It is undeniable that in some slum areas there
are bright spots where houses are occupied by the
owners and are sanitary and properly maintained.
Because of their environment, however, they have
in many cases been condemned and the properties
practically confiscated, the compensation paid being
a merely nominal sum based upon an arbitrary valuation of the site stripped of all buildings. Many
cruel hardships have resulted, and there has been
generated a natural reluctance of an important
section of public opinion to co-operate with local
authorites in slum-clearing schemes. Building
societies have no brief for slum properties, but
an amendment of this Act, long promised, would
expedite the work of clearing and would remove a
real injustice.

"What a tremendous social service would be
rendered by our societies if their contribution to

the solution of the nation's housing problem were the speedy erection of 500,000 houses, with the consequent happiness of the occupiers and the employment of thousands of artisans in the building trades ! It would establish building societies as one of the most beneficent, progressive and self-supporting forces of modern history.

"Large sections of the building industry have expressed their willingness to take part in this work, notwithstanding that there will have to be exercised very great care in the management of properties on a rental basis when they are occupied by a class of tenant who has been used to the conditions which prevail in slumdom. Every builder of, or investor in, houses to be let will desire to avoid the re-creation of slum conditions. The terms agreed to by the Association with regard to the loans, interest, and repayment period constitute a gesture of good-will and concern for the general welfare of the country.

"The scheme will constitute a test of the capacity of private enterprise and the building trade to provide the housing accommodation necessary. If they fail to put the provision of homes upon a more economic basis with a more adequate supply than has prevailed lately, the alternative will be a return to municipal building, with its grievous burden of subsidies and rates upon our industries.

"The Housing Act will naturally have its opponents. It has already been described by one writer in a newspaper as a 'colossal piece of folly on the part of the Government', and alleged that the gross rental of a house under the scheme costing £350 would involve the payment of thirteen shillings per week. I do not endorse these figures, but they are a sign that the friends of subsidised houses are vocal, if not fair. Those who live in houses should be able to pay the wages and costs of those who build them. But how can this be brought about?

"There will still be great scope for the operations of local authorities, who, with the assistance of the generous subsidies available under the Act of 1930, may provide alternative accommodation to tenants who are transferred from slums, and this subsidy will in normal cases be equivalent to five shillings a week reduction from an economic rent. This will assist the poorest section of the community."

The Housing Act of 1933 was an extension of the Housing Act of 1925, and related only to houses of not less than the minimum dimensions prescribed in that Act, namely, (a) in the case of a two-storied house, 620 superficial feet, or (b) in the case of a structurally separate and self-contained flat or a one-storied house, 550 superficial feet. The maximum dimensions laid down in the 1925 Act are 800 superficial feet in the case of a three-bedroomed and 700 feet in the case of a two-bedroomed house. The density of the houses must not exceed twelve to the acre.

The Act of 1933 in effect abolished housing

subsidies, with certain exceptions, chiefly relating to slum clearance, and made provision for the Ministry of Health, where houses of prescribed size were provided to let to persons of the working class, to share equally with the local authority and the building society the risk involved by making advances up to 90 per cent of the valuation instead of the usual 70 per cent. In other words, of the 20 per cent loan above the amount that would be normally granted, the Government, the local authority and the building society each took a third of the risk. A further concession was made as to the currency of the loan, which was to be for a period of thirty years, while the interest rates to be charged were $4\frac{1}{2}$ per cent in London and the southern counties and 4 per cent elsewhere.

It was hoped that with the aid of these attractive terms and the fall in the cost of house-construction the private investor and builder would be induced to enter the market and put up houses to let as a satisfactory investment. For its effectiveness the Act relied upon the support of four interests—the State, the local authorities, the building societies and the builder. But at each of these points certain checks were encountered.

A maximum density of twelve houses to the acre, rigidly insisted upon by the Ministry, served as a deterrent to the builders when called upon to work within so low a price-limit.

On the part of local authorities there has been a

manifest reluctance to give the guarantee required under the Act, many feeling that their support should be reserved for their own building schemes. Manchester City Council introduced a number of conditions into their guarantee, and their example was followed by other important municipalities. Attempts to solve these problems were made at joint meetings between representatives of the local authorities, the building industry and building societies, but the result was not encouraging.

As far as the building societies themselves are concerned a recent enquiry showed that a large proportion had had no proposals either to refuse or entertain. It cannot be said, however, that any great disappointment has been exhibited. The terms for the societies were not attractive, and were in fact only possible on the assumption that societies would be able to secure capital at very cheap rates over a prolonged period. Moreover, the concessions they had already made to ordinary borrowers, combined with the fall in the cost of building, had revived the demand for normal loans from owner-occupiers. In the twelve months ended September, 1933, 169,000 houses were built by private enterprise, of which 82 per cent were for sale to occupiers. The anxiety which some societies had felt as to finding an outlet for their growing funds was in consequence diminished, and during 1933 the incidence of increasing receipts and decreasing loans, marked in 1932, disappeared.

To builders the prospect of sinking 10 per cent of

the capital required in each house was not particularly attractive and in some cases not even possible; and as the demand for houses for sale outright was found to be expanding, their energies were concentrated in that direction.

The Halifax Building Society itself strongly supported the Act and pledged itself to provide £10,000,000 over a short period for those willing to erect houses to let in accordance with the terms of the Act. So far the Society has accepted or has under favourable consideration applications for financing the erection of 4,130 houses, entailing a total amount of mortgage loans of £1,290,303. The Society has also issued a booklet setting out the scope and attractions of the scheme. It is pointed out that outside London and the southern counties a payment of £5 15s. 1d. per annum for each £100 borrowed would cover interest payments and redemption for the agreed period of thirty years. In the case of a £300 house, on which £270 would be lent, this payment is equivalent to £15 10s. 9d. per annum, or approximately 6s. per week. Within London and the southern counties the annual payment to cover interest and redemption of the loan on a £400 house would be £21 19s. 9d. or 8s. 6d. per week.

Sir Enoch himself has demonstrated his faith in the workability of the Act by joining with a few friends in the erection of forty houses at Hipperholme, near Halifax, to be let in accordance with the terms of the scheme. These houses are as attractively designed and equipped as it is possible to make them, for

Sir Enoch would endorse Wells's dictum that compared with the modern house the house of a hundred years ago is half-way back to the cave !

But, when all is said, the problem of providing decent housing accommodation for the poorer classes still awaits solution. The next move is with the Government. The possibility of applying the building society principle of house-ownership may receive renewed consideration. Whatever its practicability it is a solution which carries its own commendation; for not only would houses be provided for those who need them, but a class of people whose indigence had hitherto prevented them from acquiring any considerable resources would in time find themselves possessed of the asset represented by their own homes.

Not once but scores of times do the records of building societies bear testimony to the "start" which enterprising men have made through being able to raise capital on the house they had bought. Many successful businesses which have contributed to the expansion of industry and employment have had their origin in membership of a building society. Initiative is not the prerogative of any class, but the poverty which precludes a large number of people from exercising it represents a direct loss to the community.

The application of the building society principle to the solution of this problem of the provision of houses for the poorer classes seems therefore to possess great possibilities for social and economic progress. But this is looking ahead rather than at the immediate problem, which clamours for solution.

The housing shortage has both its quantitative and qualitative aspects, and the distinction is of practical importance in the shaping of policy. The Government has announced that as a result of its invitation to local authorities to submit plans for slum clearance with the aid of the Greenwood subsidy, 1,240,182 people will be rehoused in some five years. The number of houses to be demolished is 266,851, in replacement of which 285,189 will be constructed.

While these figures indicate the prospect of a substantial improvement in the quality of house accommodation for the poorest section of the community, they make very little contribution towards the relief of the housing shortage—the quantitative aspect of the problem. The figure of Sir E. D. Simon quoted above indicate the need for over 800,000 additional houses to meet the existing shortage. So long as widespread overcrowding continues, slum clearance can do little but substitute one set of slums for another.

The Government has evidently recognized the cogency of the case for more as well as better housing accommodation, and has announced plans for rehousing displaced tenants at or near the sites of the original houses. Such accommodation will be additional to the local authorities' schemes, and a subsidy from the Exchequer will be granted, though the terms and amount are not yet known. In view of the restricted amount of space available on sites near the centre of towns, where many slum areas are situated, building upwards in flats is proposed.

In the next few years housing is thus clearly going to occupy the centre of the stage of social endeavour. The achievements of the Building Societies in their own sphere have been so remarkably effective that a certain scepticism concerning the practicability of large-scale housing subventions is inevitably encountered within the movement. All that can now be said is that time is the essence of the problem, and for a disease that will not wait for a cure the quick remedy is the one most likely to find favour.

CHAPTER XI

LOOKING FORWARD

IT is a wild day in January and the wind is sweeping down from the sombre Pennines upon Willow Hall, where it beats with crescendo fury, recedes with a sob as if in defeat and returns reinforced to its battery of walls which have withstood it for three hundred years.

Riding on the moods of the wind, the rain swishes round the eaves and sinks into a patter, till it is caught up again and tossed wildly across the glistening landscape. It is decidedly a day to be indoors, to gather around roaring fires, and pity less fortunate mortals whose duties have kept them abroad. So let us leave the storm outside and fly for sanctuary to the sitting-room at Willow Hall, where the fire burns brightly, discovering aventurine depths in the panelled walls.

In one corner a grandfather clock—a present to Sir Enoch from the staff of the Halifax Society—looks down benignly. Lady Hill is crocheting, seated in a low chair before the fire, with the cotton rolled away from her knee across the hearth. A movement to recover it she discourages with a smile. Sir Enoch is settled comfortably opposite her, talking, and seemingly giving a good deal of attention to keeping his pipe alight, though his thoughts are absorbed by what he is saying. The conversation has been on the development of the work of the Building Society movement, and after a pause Sir Enoch goes on:

" I have every confidence that the future of the Building Society movement is one of success and usefulness. There is such a definite—and I am afraid increasing—shortage of houses that even when all efforts in prospect to provide houses for occupation by tenants have been completed there will still be a very great field available for the assistance of those who desire to become owners of their homes.

"There is an innate desire and ambition in a large proportion of our best citizen-workers to become owners of homes, not only as an expression of independence and individualism, but also as a means of acquiring capital and a house free from debt for the middle or later part of their lives. Every slum area demolished will unhouse some proportion of people who will wish to become home-owners rather than to be transferred to a municipally erected and controlled dwelling on a tenancy basis.

"At the same time, builders will always prefer to build houses for sale, because they can turn over their capital again and again, and go on producing houses, as other goods are produced, for sale.

"One other significant incentive to home-ownership is the growing appreciation of the importance of design. The activities of the modern architect have done much to raise the general taste to a fairly high level; and personal taste can be satisfied best through ownership."

"Although the first business of building societies is

with the value of the property on which they are asked to lend, have they not," Sir Enoch was asked, "a moral responsibility to exert their immense influence for the preservation of the amenities of the country-side?"

"The primary duty of building societies is to make loans upon good security in the interests of their investors," Sir Enoch replied, "and they may be relied upon to carry out this duty. But they have, I agree, an obligation to assist prospective house-purchasers with their advice. I do not think, however, that the responsibility for choice of site or design should be laid upon the societies. Borrowers must be free to satisfy their own desires as to the design of the houses they purchase. But they should certainly be careful to obtain advice from skilled valuers as to the price which they ought to pay for the kind of house they want.

"In this connection they may have the assurance that the building societies will continue to employ professional surveyors and valuers, with high qualifications and local knowledge. Their valuations can be relied upon—to the extent of 99 per cent, in fact—and this protects the interests of the purchaser. But over choice of site or design the societies have no control."

"What is the societies' attitude towards 'ribbon' building?"

" A good deal of attention has been given to the question of ribbon building—this regrettable practice of building along the margins of high-roads. I have advocated, in public speeches, the alternative of developing land farther away from the high-roads, where not only would land be cheaper, but there would be quiet, greater safety for children, and freedom from the dust and disturbance of constantly running traffic. The ideal solution seems to me to be the development of such estates, planned by architects who would build houses of attractively varying design while retaining a unity of conception for each estate."

"What will be the consequences if the present low rates of interest continue?"

"A hopeful portent for the future of building societies is the continued cheapness of capital. There is a definite tendency for rates of interest to be reduced, and the cost of home-ownership will be correspondingly cheaper, and so more attractive to an increasing number of people. This tendency will receive every possible encouragement from building society managers, who regard low rates of interest as a very important attraction, as well as an assistance, to house-purchasers. Low rates of interest to borrowers will, of course, mean that lower rates will be paid to investing members, but it is obvious that between the two much less hardship will be suffered by investors receiving a lower rate than by borrowers being charged a higher rate of interest; for in the one case the rate of interest represents merely an accretion to capital, whereas in the case of borrowers a lower rate of interest means a lower cost of house accommodation, and often the difference between practicable and impracticable desire

for ownership. The workability of low rates of interest
has been illustrated, I think, by the experience of the
six largest banks of the country during the half year
which ended on December 31st last. It has been
notorious that rates of interest allowed by banks upon
deposits have been almost infinitesimal in many cases,
and in practically every instance, I imagine, there has
been a very substantial reduction in the rate of interest
allowed to depositors. Notwithstanding this, the profits have been on the whole considerably increased, and
essential margins for the successful conduct of the
business of the banks have been provided.

"Of course, banks occupy a position quite different
from that of the building societies. Someone has said
that a banker's first duty is to know the difference
between a bill and a mortgage. Bankers must keep
the bulk of their assets in liquid, or at any rate easily
recallable, form, as quite half of their liabilities to
their depositors are payable on demand and the rest
on very short notice. Deposit banking and the provision of long-term capital cannot therefore be
reconciled.

"For this reason I do not think that the banks, as
such, have much contribution to make to the building
up of a much-needed organisation to provide fixed
capital for the medium borrower. The large borrower
is provided for by the ordinary facilities of the new
issues market, but a small, enterprising business man
must usually look to his friends, or find someone to
'back' him, which is not always possible. The

consequence is that much enterprise that would be both practical and profitable, and of assistance to the community, enters the list of hopes deferred and wastes itself away.

"What is the remedy? I advocate the setting up of a public fund, financed by the Government, out of which men and women with reasonable propositions would be provided with capital. The security would be the plant, buildings or stock purchased by the borrowers, in regard to which the principle adopted in the Bills of Sale Act could be applied. Failure and loss would be encountered, but clearly this would be only in the minority of cases; and as the fund would be self-supporting, provision for possible losses would be made in the rate of interest charged to all borrowers, and this could still be low enough to be attractive. The fund would be kept free from all political influence by being operated on the approved public board principle, with a carefully selected personnel of men of business ability and acumen.

"The encouragement of many thousands who have all the skill and initiative, but no money, would be of immense indirect benefit to the State. Unemployment would be reduced and taxable profits increased, while socially a feeling of injustice would be removed. Those who feel handicapped by lack of capital would no longer be left to derive consolation only from the contemplation of others, apparently with plenty, making little use of it.

"One other aspect of this proposition requires

consideration, I think. Future outlets for new capital on the grand scale of the past may not recur. The opening up of undeveloped countries has now proceeded far. We must expect a permanent contraction in overseas lending operations—and some will not regard it as anything to be regretted, for much money lent abroad could have been more profitably used at home. In those numerous cases in which overseas borrowers have defaulted, the loans we made simply represent a loss of real wealth to this country. Yet so many apparently believe that for prosperity we must achieve a 'favourable' trade balance—which, of course, is simply another way of saying that our total exports must exceed our imports and the gap be filled by our loans—that it is perhaps providential that we should find this method of getting rid of our wealth in exchange for debt no longer practicable. The fact is that in the past foreign borrowers have been served by a much more effective organisation than home borrowers, and that has had much to do with the way things have gone.

"It is significant that in the seven years ended 1931 this country lent to overseas borrowers £819,000,000, while the sum of our favourable balances on income account in these years was £577,000,000, which indicates that we had lent £242,000,000 more than was justified by our trade position; and also that the people to whom we lent preferred to spend a good deal of our money in purchases from other countries.

"Yes, I agree that this was largely because the

over-valuation of the pound under our return to the Gold Standard at the old parity had rendered our goods unattractive in price; but is it not a curious reflection that all this over-lending was allowed when our export trade was incapacitated in this manner, while to-day, when its competitive power is fully restored, overseas lending is rigidly checked?

"But whether overseas lending is a virtue or a vice is not so much the point as that in the future, even when something approaching normal economic conditions is restored, we shall not be able to indulge in it so extensively as in the past. But with this outlet for the nation's savings partly dammed, others must be opened so that no part of the total may be allowed to form into idle pools with adverse effect on trade and prices. Savings that formerly went to finance a favourable export balance must now be turned to irrigate the fields of home industry. But it won't be one by wishing. . . . And so I suggest the formation of this publicly controlled fund to meet a real economic need. As one who is responsible for the control and management of many millions of public money, I say unhesitatingly that this scheme is sound and practicable.

"It should not be forgotten that, through the operation of building societies, capital is often provided for industrial and business purposes. From my own experience I could quote scores of examples of prosperous businesses being built up from the capital first made available either through a house purchased by means of a building society loan and redeemed in the ordinary way or through the accumulation of savings in monthly subscription shares.

"As an example of what can be done by regular saving I may mention a local Congregational minister who died recently at an advanced age. He was, needless to say, very poorly paid, but in his lifetime he completed a series of subscription shares three times, and when he died left £17,000 in the Halifax Building Society.

"But among the most interesting cases I have ever known of the profitable application of building society thrift is one that occurred as long ago as 1898. It was recounted at a Building Society Conference at Bradford—one of the first ever held. Mr. Charles Higham, secretary of the St. Bride's and City of London Building Society, had prepared a paper for the conference, giving some account of his long experience of building society work, and in the course of his paper he said—well, perhaps I can do no better than read you Mr. Higham's exact words as they were published in the record of the conference:

"'Among the persons I advised to join the St. Bride's Society was a shopman at a printer's in Shoe Lane. This man, being also interested in a business in Poppin's Court, Fleet Street, was able to save £2 per month, which he continued to do until the principal and interest amounted to about £200, when he told me he wished to withdraw. I inquired what he intended to do with the money, and he replied, "Buy a ninth share in the *Daily Telegraph*"—which he did. It may not be generally known that the *Daily Telegraph* was established by Colonel Sleigh, who became bankrupt, and the assignee had great difficulty in finding a purchaser, but he eventually sold it for £1,800. The last time I saw the person I refer to—which was about thirty years ago—he told me that his £200 brought in £2,000 per annum, and I have no doubt that whoever may now be the fortunate owner of that share receives £15,000 or £20,000 per annum for it!'

"While that is obviously a spectacular and exceptional instance of the advantageous use of savings, I often hear of people who established their fortunes on the foundation of capital saved with the assistance of a building society. Recently I attended a public luncheon at Canterbury, and in my speech mentioned this aspect of building society work. Sir William Wayland, the Member of Parliament for the division, who spoke after me, expressed his personal interest in my observation, saying he himself had first raised the capital to engage in business on the strength of a house he had bought through a building society.

"One other development which is going to be of increasing importance in the economic life of the nation, but which I do not think has received much notice: I refer to the fact that we are now entering the period in which the first batch of houses erected under the great post-war expansion in building society lending

activities is becoming fully paid for. In 1919 the
building societies advanced nearly £16,000,000 for
house-purchase. It has gone on expanding, and now
some £90,000,000 a year is being so advanced. Many
thousands of the houses erected in 1919 and 1920
and 1921 were bought under repayment agreements
covering a period of from fourteen to fifteen years.
In 1934 there will be some 80,000 houses freed from
all rent or mortgage payments, and the owners will
be, in consequence, able to afford a higher standard
of living. And the number will increase rapidly.

"Of course, saving habits acquired over a long
period tend to perpetuate themselves, but it is un-
questionable that thousands of people will now buy
things which they have previously denied themselves,
and demand will be stimulated in many directions.

"It is true that repayments of borrowers do not lie
idle in building societies, but flow out again in fresh
loans for the purchase of houses, but this lending
process will not be restricted, as the societies are
secure in their supply of resources. The expenditure
of those no longer paying instalments to building
societies will thus constitute an addition to the demand
for goods.

"The future of the Housing Act of 1933 is uncertain,
but not unhopeful. The chief impediment to its
operations has been the restrictions imposed by local
authorities. It is, of course, obvious that building
societies themselves cannot take the initiative, as they
do not engage directly in building operations. Their

part is to be prepared to help when approached by those prepared to build. You are aware of the steps taken by the Halifax Society to assist the operations of the Act, and most of the other leading societies are equally anxious to co-operate. If this scheme fails, there is a prospect of a return to the old method of subsidised building, which has proved expensive and wasteful.

"Although the Registrar's report will not be ready for a few months, it will show that the building societies made further headway in 1933, and that the total assets are now in excess of £500,000,000. When about eighteen months ago the demand for loans showed signs of falling off, many thought the progress of the movement was to receive a check. But an examination of the figures for 1933 will show that the societies are finding no difficulty in the employment of their resources in the normal manner. Some 850,000 houses are now being purchased through building societies.

"But in its widest aspect the improvement in general housing conditions depends upon the success with which we tackle the grave economic problems still confronting us. So long as people have not the money to pay for decent accommodation, the task of providing it will be slow, uphill work, amid all kinds of discouragement. Upon the establishment of more prosperous conditions, particularly for what are now the poorest classes, a good deal of our hope must therefore rest."

Sir Enoch muses a while, and lights his pipe again.

"It is possible to derive some confidence in the future," he adds, "from the fact that most of the present hardship and deprivation is not inevitable, but the result of defective economic organisation, and therefore it is capable of remedy. The success of the Building Society movement is essentially the result of adjustment of means to ends, and an example of what can be achieved by an orderly use of our economic resources. Without such an organisation one can picture circumstances in which people might desire to borrow for the purpose of buying their houses and be willing to pay interest on the loans, while others might be able and willing to lend and receive interest; but with none to weld together these complementary desires there would be no house-purchase, no borrowers and no interest.

"Is the picture so fantastic?" Sir Enoch goes on. "Not if we remember that there are to-day millions who desire to work, millions who urgently need the goods their work would produce, idle plant ready to be set in operation, raw materials that are being destroyed or restricted in production, and idle money awaiting investment—every single element seeking a satisfaction that some other is eager to fulfil.

"We cannot, of course, turn round and say that a system exhibiting these defects is incapable of giving better results. History would defy such an assertion. I have no doubt that individual enterprise, combined with social safeguards where the need is indicated, remains the most satisfactory basis, economically and psychologically, upon which to build our future prosperity. But that is far from saying that things have only to be left alone and all will be well. The future is not with those who hope to muddle through or who rely vaguely on some such inaccurate analogy as the 'swing of the pendulum'.

"I believe that we shall have to submit our economic organisation to a scientific overhaul before we can hope to enjoy to the full the benefits of the increasing productivity of industry and agriculture. To destroy commodities, or even to restrict production, is an admission of defeat. We must not be eager to cover up economic defects when they are revealed—and there can be no doubt that the stress of recent years has discovered defects which call insistently for remedy.

"One is the behaviour of the monetary system. Commodity prices have plunged downward, not because goods are cheaper to produce, but because the monetary demand for them has fallen off. Over large fields of industry and agriculture, producers have not been able to cover costs of production, and although industry has been able partly to meet the situation by closing down or reducing production—at the cost of heavy unemployment—agriculturists have had inevitably to go on producing even at ruinous prices, and countries primarily dependent on agriculture have been brought to the verge of bankruptcy.

"The world is learning that cheapness resulting from changes in the purchasing power of money, as distinct from that which comes from more economical methods of production, brings disaster in its train. The primary need, therefore, is a monetary system stable in terms of commodities, within which, of course, individual prices would vary according to the supply of and demand for them. But the general level of prices—which is simply the value of money—would remain stable, except to the extent that the purchasing power of money was very gradually increased by increasing industrial efficiency.

"If the monetary system is working properly, increased production should present no terrors, nor should the increased use of mechanical appliances. People sometimes talk as if we had only begun to use machines in 1929. The demand for goods is created by the production of goods—all the items grouped under the heading of 'Costs of Production' being somebody's income. If, therefore, those incomes all come to market again, the total monetary demand for goods will always be sufficient to carry off their output.

"The trouble arises when the income created by the production of goods and the rendering of service do not all return to market to carry off those goods and services. And this is what has happened in recent years.

"It must be remembered that the incomes arising from current economic activity provide both the means of current expenditure and the means of saving. And saving may or may not pass into circulation.

When, for example, a thrifty man puts away a pound a week in a building society he has to reduce his standard of living to that extent, and so, as a purchaser, his demand is minus a pound a week. Now imagine tens of thousands of people all doing this—wage-earners producing goods whose wages are embodied in the price of the goods, but whose wages are not wholly being spent in the purchase of those goods. It might seem, at first glance, that here is a potent influence against the demand for goods being equal to their supply, leading therefore to a fall in prices.

"But this is not so, because the building societies pass on the savings, and they emerge in current purchasing power in the hands of bricklayers, plasterers, joiners, decorators, and hosts of others, who thus in effect are given power to consume what the savers, in their abstinence, have refrained from consuming.

"We see, therefore, that both saving and spending contribute to current demand, the former equally passing into circulation as current purchasing power in the hands of those producing durable or capital goods. But a situation may arise—has in fact arisen in recent years—where this smooth working of the economic organisation is disrupted.

"If, for one reason or another, the demand for capital goods falls off, the avenue through which saved resources flow back into the stream of current purchasing power is immediately blocked. Saving goes on—though its volume is gradually reduced by the spread of depression—but the money so saved goes to swell bank deposits and the demand for existing Stock Exchange securities. It does not pass back into current circulation, and the diminution of demand on the part of those who save is not compensated for by the transfer of this demand to the hands of those who borrow and spend their borrowings on the construction of capital goods. A fall in current demand and prices is therefore inevitable.

"Now the building societies have clearly played an important role in keeping that part of the nation's savings which reaches them flowing back into circulation, and to that extent has done something to mitigate the fall in commodity prices. But the catastrophic decline in the output of such capital goods as ships, railway engines, machines and plants of all kinds, and the construction of new factories—by means of which 'saved' money was put back into current circulation—indicates only too clearly the cause of the decline in prices and demand.

"The need for the stimulation of capital expenditure is therefore apparent, and emphasises the desirability of the Government's taking action to put capital resources, which may otherwise lie idle, at the disposal of those who will use them, first to *purchase* capital equipment, so turning the loans they receive into current purchasing power to the benefit of the community, and second to *operate* this 'capital' equipment to the inevitable benefit of trade, industry and employment.

"Until we have some degree of equilibrium restored

between costs and prices I think we must avoid the rigidities of the Gold Standard, the abandonment of which has proved of great benefit to this country. Stability of foreign exchanges is desirable, but the first consideration must be stability of purchasing power of the currency at a level permitting costs to be covered by prices, for this sort of stability, and not that which concerns foreign currencies, is the influence determining industrial prosperity or the reverse. Industry can go to pieces with stable exchanges, as was seen in the two years prior to our abandonment of the Gold Standard, but it will never relapse when the purchasing power of money is stable. There are also questions of social justice as between various classes of the community which will not be settled until the value of money in terms of real wealth possesses some reasonable assurance of stability—but into these I shall not go. No doubt you will be thinking I am never going to stop."

Sir Enoch rises to knock the ashes from his pipe into the embers now burning low. The hands of the grandfather clock show that the night is well advanced, and it is time to bid farewell to the hospitable walls of Willow Hall.

A little later, and Sir Enoch's car is at the door. It moves smoothly and swiftly towards the lights of Halifax below. The soft cushions invite relaxation, and inevitably reflection turns on the life of the man who, once a silk-spinner's boy, can now send his guests home in such luxurious fashion. Men in great places, wrote Francis Bacon, are thrice servants— servants of the State; servants of fame; servants of business.

And may not one add that Enoch Hill, among them, has been twice blessed?—for his own enjoyment of success and the "great places" has gone always hand in hand with benefit given to other people. When he had no other gift to make, he gave himself. His look has been turned ever outward; and however rough the path, his step has never faltered nor his faith been shaken. And a life which, more than most, has seen its aspirations realised and its hopes fulfilled, is now, in its fourteenth lustre, still looking forward, still finding plans to make, service to give and work to do.

Work! Is that Sir Enoch's secret? How disappointing!

Well, perhaps work and something else. Not luck at any rate. Most men would go far to avoid the luck that imposed upon Hill so many handicaps at the start. We are driven to compromise on character, developed through a fortunate inheritance and environment. Those indeed have been great possessions, and of them Enoch Hill has been a wise steward.

THE END